Love Talk

A Communication Guide for Married Couples

Eugene F. Stehura, Ph.D.

Sheed & Ward

Sheed & Ward™ is a service of National Catholic Reporter Publishing Company, Inc.

Library of Congress Catalog Card Number: 90-62652

ISBN: 1-55612-403-1

Published by: Sheed & Ward
                 115 E. Armour Blvd. P.O. Box 419492
                 Kansas City, MO 64141-6492

To order, call: (800) 333-7373

Contents

INTRODUCTION

The day after returning home from my honeymoon, I counseled my first couple with marital problems. In the course of the last 20 years, I have been able to witness both the manner in which conflicts arise and develop between husbands and wives, as well as the ways in which these problems were resolved. I have also learned, through my own marriage, about the difficulties couples incur in communicating with one another, and the rewards of working through those barriers that each of us erects to a more intimate relationship. I have also seen that when couples decide to face and admit their own contributions to their marital discord, a closeness to self begins to occur, which, in turn, spawns a deeper intimacy in the marriage. I have seen that when couples apply new behaviors to old conflictual habits, tension quickly subsides, hope is engendered, and previous intimacy returns.

My role as a psychologist is to teach couples to speak therapeutically to one another; that is, to share their feelings, needs, strengths and weaknesses, rather than point out the deficiencies and failures of their spouse. The language of combat and control must be replaced by the language of love and sharing. In this book, I want to share the insights and techniques that I have found to be helpful to the many couples that I have been privileged to serve through counseling.

Throughout my professional experience, I have also observed that men and women are able to speak easily and tirelessly with one another while dating. Early in their marriage, communication also seems to occur without much effort. Gradually, however, as the marriage wears on, couples often begin to lose this facility for communicating comfortably with one another. Yet husbands, who can talk so freely with the neighbor about sports, cars, or household projects, may be unable to calmly discuss with their wives such topics as child rearing, work in or around the home, or the handling of finances. Wives, on the other hand, feel understood so readily and talk so intimately with other women about children, personal health, and plans for the future, but they can find it difficult to connect with their husbands.

It is not that couples cannot communicate. It is rather that unique difficulties arise when they actually take the time to talk through important matters affecting their lives. They often do not understand why communication problems always seem to crop up, but beyond that, how to deal with them when they do. It is in response to these two concerns that this book has been written.

This book may also be useful to couples who feel their communication is open and effective, and who desire further growth and development. In addition to exploring basic communication techniques, a three-fold plan will be discussed and presented to every married couple: to convey understanding, to impart knowledge, and to offer a challenge to consider effective communication as an essential part of a healthy marriage.

First, couples will hopefully come to understand that problems in marital communication are normal. All marriages experience them. Without conflict, the desire and motivation to find solutions and reach for deeper intimacy might be thwarted. Without frustration, a relationship might stagnate, suffer boredom, or fail to reach its potential. Conflicts stimulate new growth. Conflicts also keep couples grounded in their humanness, and in their need to reach out for help and change.

Secondly, all couples need a clear vision of the most common problem areas in marital communication, how they originate, escalate, but more importantly, how these very problems can eventually be transformed into exciting solutions and avenues for deeper intimacy. The chapter on "Communication Stoppers" describes nine ways of preventing a meaningful exchange from occurring, while the chapter on "Communication Starters" discusses twelve ways to repair and enhance dialogue in the future.

Finally, each couple will be challenged to change their own relationship by learning and initiating specific Communication Starters that apply particularly to them. Spontaneous impulsivity and mood-dominated behavior will give way to a deliberate and calmly-controlled manner of beginning a conversation. This, hopefully, will spur new levels of confidence and excitement where each couple can make effective and positive communication happen any time they want, because they now possess the tools and knowledge to promote open and flowing discussion.

CHAPTER I

Communication Is Work!

Communication is work because it takes time, effort, and energy. Spouses who work long days are tired at night. The last thing they want is more work, like a serious conversation. It is easier to avoid communicating in favor of reading a book, watching television, or doing a hobby. Yet, if a plant does not have sun and water, it will die. The same is true for a relationship. If it is not fed by meaningful and frequent conversation, it will slowly wither, starve, and eventually die into silence. Talking reveals as well as unites. Talking expresses as well as enkindles love. Talking can build a marriage, but if left undone, it can tear a marriage down. Anyone can talk. But talking with love is not as easy as it may seem. It requires self-reflection and self-control. Each spouse must learn to master his or her own spontaneity, impulsiveness, and conquer those negative habits that perhaps were brought with them into marriage. Old behaviors must weaken so new behaviors can arise and be developed. Only then will communication between spouses become an encounter that unites two separate individuals into an intimacy of real oneness.

Marital communication may be described as an art, in that it requires skill and practice; or a science, in that it requires knowledge and technique. The content of marital communication can be extrinsic: about external, relevant, but uncritical areas of concern, such as the need for entertainment, diversion, material things, or news events. Communication can also be intrinsic: about internal, personal matters of importance to one or both spouses, such as the need for sharing, affection, understanding, and intimacy, as well as the need for a home, children, or career development. Intrinsic communication offers various levels of openness and invites each spouse to explore previously-closed levels of vulnerability.

A model of vibrant, alive communication in marriage is one in which each spouse is free to communicate on different levels of personal self-disclosure, as his or her need presents itself. Talking about extrinsic matters is as necessary as talking about intrinsic concerns. Too much seriousness is as detrimental as too much superficiality. There is a time for what is personal and a time for what is playful, a time for crying and a time for laughing. Good communication has this complementary polarity.

On the other hand, poor communication can be seen as just the opposite, a unipolar rigidity. This means that communication becomes skewed and lopsided, comfortable when talking about some matters and strained when discussing others. Emotional subjects are avoided. One spouse often feels controlled or shut out by the other. Since important issues are not discussed and resolved, conflicts and tensions can gradually infiltrate the relationship. Fear replaces joy, anger replaces love, coldness replaces warmth. Instead of a spontaneous freedom to share both the trivial and the personal, there exists a rigid attempt to control communication and thereby avoid exposing the most vulnerable part of one's self, those needs and hurts buried deep in the heart.

Dysfunctional communication seems to just happen in most marriages. No spouse needs training in the art of provoking a fight, retaliating for being hurt, or trying to control the other through the various and creative forms of intimidation. Poor communication just happens. It can occur when the impulse to speak governs the timing of communication, when the mood of the moment governs the content, or when the feeling toward the other governs the tone of delivery. If what is said, when it is said, and how it is said is not deliberately monitored and controlled, communication can quickly break down. Good communication, on the other hand, must be learned and practiced. If it is initiated with consideration and gentleness, any discussion can blossom into a moment of togetherness.

CHAPTER II

Language Differences Between Husbands and Wives

In the many years of counseling couples, I have been aware that each spouse speaks a different language from the other, and this can cause an inherent tension in their relationship. There are two ways that couples seek to resolve this situation. First, one spouse may try to make the other speak his or her language. "You do the changing, act the way I want, and we will get along better." This solution simply does not work, and only more conflict will ensue. After all, no spouse wants to be told how to behave.

A second solution can occur when each spouse attempts to value, understand, and speak the language of the other. "I will try to speak more calmly and to the point so that you will enjoy my communication, and you in turn will talk about your feelings so that I can become closer to you through your sharing." By learning to speak a new language, each spouse can expand and develop a new but previously hidden part of his/herself, thereby becoming more complete and fulfilled. It is only when each individual decides to personally change and grow that the relationship also will begin to rise to new and exciting dimensions. Now let us discuss these language differences.

There are five major language styles that couples use: namely, few vs. many-wordedness, personal vs. objective sharing,

4

emotional vs. detached discussing, now vs. later tactics, and literal vs. implied interpretation.

Few vs. Many-Wordedness

Marital communication can be both deeply meaningful and rewarding as well as hurtful and straining. Difficulties arise because of the different ways spouses speak to one another. One spouse might be brief, to the point, objective, "only the facts, please." This spouse is inclined to conserve energy, time and their own self for concrete accomplishments or non-personal pursuits. Too much talking may threaten emotional arousal, risk the loss of affective control, or lead to self-disclosure. The other spouse may be verbose, detailed, talking all around a point before saying it. That spouse thinks out loud. Time for talking is necessary for their subjective awakenings to become translated into understandable views and opinions. Tension will inevitably form between these spouses. "Why can't she just talk to me and get to the point?" or "Why doesn't he understand how to communicate with me?" each spouse laments. "Communication would be so much easier if we just talked alike!"

Personal vs. Objective Sharing

Two people are bound to come into marriage with differences in their communication styles. One spouse may be feeling and relationship-oriented, and focuses on what the other is experiencing. This spouse may need to have an "airing out of feelings" in order to bring his or her equilibrium into balance. But this may serve to disturb the other spouse, who contracts at the mention of emotion. That spouse feels at home when discussing responsibilities, getting things done, caring for the home, or the concrete planning of future necessities.

Each spouse struggles to maintain his or her unipolar rigidity. Changing one's spouse seems easier than changing one's self. In a marriage relationship, each one will usually test to see if the other can be changed.

Emotional vs. Detached Discussion

Another difference centers around the cool-hot approach to communication. One spouse can aggravate the other by remaining cool, reasonable, objective, and unemotional in the field of battle. The heated spouse can become more frustrated, and may try to elicit some arousal of emotion in the other. Openly fighting makes the relationship feel more real and may lead to a resolution of the problem. But too often, emotions become overdramatized and intensified in order to punish, teach, or intimidate the more detached spouse, thereby preventing a genuine sharing and closeness from occurring.

On the other hand, the stay-calm spouse can become exasperated by an intense display of feelings, and tries to remain placid in order to tranquilize the other. The cool spouse attempts to avoid conflict, to retreat from the struggle for intimacy, and to focus on the surface and extrinsic, rather than look inward and stir up the depths of his or her personal vulnerabilities.

Now vs. Later Tactics

Added pitfalls arise over the timing of household responsibilities. The work-rest controversy wiggles its way into most marriages after a few years. Upon coming home from a long day of hard work, one spouse falls into the chair in front of the television. His or her first thought is, "Relax now, work later! Recharge that dead battery! It's time for me!" But this attempt at solitary hibernation for one spouse may negatively excite the work-oriented spouse, who sees only what still needs to be done around the house. *Rigor mortis* should set in after death, not after coming home from work. The compulsive spouse cannot relax until all the work is done. But since all the work never has been nor ever will be completely finished, he or she can seldom relax. While this spouse outlines new jobs to be undertaken and finds work in every corner, the "relaxing" spouse may shrink into some hidden corner of the sofa, hoping for a few moments of undisturbed, guilt-free leisure. "Work should be rewarded with rest" is the first thought. "Cleanliness is next to godliness," or "Order is its own reward," are not enough to move this spouse from his or her comfortable recline. From this relationship, an attacking, passive-aggressive style of communication arises. The "worker" spouse is always on the alert, trying to motivate the other NOW. The "resting" spouse responds with a grumbling noncompliance or a half-hearted attempt to appease the other LATER.

Literal vs. Implied Interpretation

Oftentimes, language differences occur in the literal vs. the inferred meaning each spouse attributes to the words they use. One spouse may hear the lines, and the other may hear what is between the lines. Confusion often occurs when one spouse speaks figuratively but the other hears literally. "Would you care to wash the dishes?" does not mean, "Would you mind doing them if you feel in the mood and have nothing else to do?" It means, "I want you to do the dishes, now. You would be helping me a lot." But if the other spouse responds literally, such as, "No, honey, I do not care to do the dishes, but thanks for asking," a minor civil war may erupt. The between-the-lines spouse bemoans, "Do I have to tell him everything? Can't he see what I need without being told? Did I marry a child?" The literal spouse laments, "I am not a mind reader. Just tell me what you want. I resent it when you expect me to read your mind."

It is clear that people have differences in the meanings they give to their words, the manner in which they deliver those words, the importance of the personal needs that underlie their words, and the frequency with which they need to speak those words. Because of the nuances surrounding the spoken word, discord will find little resistance in taking root in the communication in most marriages.

Just as language differences provoke conflict and the quest for power and control, they also can challenge couples toward a deeper self-awareness, self-control, and self-disclosure. For communication to be satisfying, the freedom to express feelings and ideas, and an ability to receive and embrace opposing views, must occur. Each spouse must reach inside and develop new ways of listening and sharing. Spontaneous impulsivity must be complemented by sensitive deliberation. Laconic self-concealing must bow to a word-filled self-disclosure. Emotional free swinging must be tempered by the gentle expression of inner feelings. It is this very movement from tension to calmness, from closedness to openness, that gives marriage excitement, aliveness, health and growth. Leaving communication the same year after year spells psychological stagnation and slow death. An unchanging life is a life unlived.

Finally, differences attract. If one spouse married an identical other, dissatisfaction would soon emerge. Since there may be much that a person dislikes in himself or herself, looking at an identical other accentuates the imperfection that he or she is trying to hide. There is the hope that by marrying someone with complimentary strengths, those desirable traits will eventually become incorporated into one's own personality. For example, an introverted husband hopes that he can become more sociable by frequent interaction with his more outgoing wife. The loquacious wife may find her husband's ability to listen attentively to others a necessary compliment to her extroversion. But, as most of us have grown to know, transformation does not take place by mere proximity, observation, or osmosis, but by self-reflection, determination, and practice.

CHAPTER III

Four Areas Where
Communication Goes Wrong

Married couples argue and disagree over many and diverse issues and problems. Relational stress is frequently experienced when couples attempt to engage in four forms of communication. By far, the most challenging areas of dialogue occur during the times of asking, discussing, expressing, or sharing. Tensions and conflicts may appear automatically the moment one spouse tries to: ask the other to do something, discuss an emotional subject, express a negative feeling, or share a positive emotion. These are the four most common types of communication. When the object of our dialogue is presented in the uniqueness of a marital relationship, then asking, discussing, expressing, and sharing become difficult in one sense, yet provide opportunities for growth in another. We will explore each one, in both their constructive and destructive forms.

If feelings did not require expression, if dependency needs were nonexistent, if problems could be solved unilaterally, conflicts in marriage would become dinosaurs of the past. But since there is a need to make what is felt inwardly visible to one's mate, and a need to work together and cooperate in order to raise a family or maintain a home, conflict will be an inherent part of every marital relationship. External conflicts produce internal tensions. The prolongation of unsettled tensions stirs up the necessary motivation that enables spouses to risk admitting failure and attempting new behavior.

1. Asking for Assistance

The moment some job needs to be done and you want your spouse to do it, tremors of anticipation can be felt throughout the marital landscape. The timing is almost always off, now versus later. One spouse views and demands that the job must be done now. The other writhes in anticipation of tension and attempts to delay the start at all costs. Instead of a simple transaction of the question, a clear response, and a resolution, what can occur is a complex dialogue of ambiguous responses that leave both parties dissatisfied. The question may be met with hedging, no commitment to a "yes" or "no," leaving a pretense of a resolution. "Pretense" is an accurate word here, because the relationship is hovering over the onset of a conflict.

The word "later" can be a safety valve for one spouse and an acidic irritant to the other. As long as the one spouse intends to do the task, without actually doing it, he or she believes that they are responsive to, and in compliance with, the other's request. Intention, not action, may be thought of as enough. Only emergencies should require an immediacy of response. What can be put off until tomorrow should be put off. Life seems work-filled and complicated enough without over-extending the work ethic to the sanctuary of one's own home.

The requesting spouse may have a different relaxation schedule. While the requested spouse relaxes by putting off work, and avoids even the thought of it, the requesting spouse may be able to relax only after work has been accomplished. It is as if the asking spouse has a radar system that spots the "left undone" and the "needs to be done" and consequently creates an agenda of "must do's." The other spouse may have a "shut off" switch by which he or she can block out the thought of work, with not the slightest temptation to consider the merit of doing a particular task at the time. The asking spouse, here, is task-centered and order-oriented. A day without accomplishing anything is a day wasted. Resting becomes justified after what "still needs to be done" is actually done. The other spouse views resting as justified when what "had to be done" was done. The "must" battles the "should" for supremacy.

The asking spouse looks to the future, envisions new goals, dreams new possibilities. This spouse can become frustrated if these ambitions are not mutual and feels restless if movement is not made toward those ends. Whether it is saving for a new home or painting a bedroom, delay or disinterest arouses an unbearable tension in the asking spouse. Love means valuing and responding to the needs of the other. When these needs are down-played, put off, or ignored, the bond of love becomes threatened and weakened.

Not only is asking for work to be done a tricky maneuver that often ends in frustation, but also requesting time for leisure and play can be punished by a guilt-producing response. No work, then no play. "How can you think of going to a ball game when there is so much to be done around the house?" The work-oriented spouse makes too little time for play, while the rest-oriented spouse makes too little time for work. Avoidance of work can be countered by denial of companionship for play. "If you refuse to work, I will refuse to play." Retaliation is a common tactic or response when one spouse feels his or her needs are being devalued. Needs are indistinguishable from the very fabric of our humanness, and when our needs are dismissed callously, we feel rejected, misunderstood, and unloved.

It seems so obviously simple that couples who love each other should have no trouble affirming and attending to each other's needs. "Ask and you will receive." Yet as the luster of romance tarnishes over time, our dormant self-interest and our desire for control can awaken. It can happen in marriage that asking becomes an occasion for tension, and the spontaneous, unstructured response becomes a fuse that ignites an explosion. If spouses never had to ask each other for help or assistance, many conflicts would be eliminated.

"Ask and you will not receive" can become an expectation. Once spouses realize that this has become the motto of their relationship, a cynical detachment or a battle-readiness appears. Marriage then becomes a contest and a conquest, instead of a co-operation and a cohesion.

2. Discussing an Emotional Subject

Trying to discuss an important issue is a second situation in which married couples experience a struggle for harmony amidst the dissonance of individual self-interest. Marriages are composed of two separate identities, with varied needs, feelings, and ideas about any given subject. Seldom do two spouses view things the exact same way. Yet without cooperation and consensus, problems remain unsolved and decisions are left unmade. Decisions that are unilaterally made without discussion, compromise, and agreement can be viewed as dictates and imperatives. At its worst, the relationship may be felt as a tyranny, lived in fear of the other. The compliant spouse can come to exist in a state of intimidation and insecurity. Discussion is unnecessary, and even useless, when one spouse must always get his or her way. In this type of relationship, closeness is replaced by power and fear.

Open and mutual discussion of important matters can thus be thwarted in two ways, by passive avoidance or by aggressive domination. In either case, mutual and loving participation by both spouses is precluded. Discussing issues in a way that is respectful of each other's feelings and ideas is necessary for the growth of marital love. Because both spouses can see the same issue differently and believe that they are usually correct, discussion all too often leads to conflict. But by responding in a deliberate and effective manner to the other spouse's ideas, conflicts can be successfully overcome.

Discussion involving intrinsic communication issues proves difficult because each spouse is emotionally involved in the problem and may want their own way. Someone has to "win" and someone must "lose." Some intrinsic concerns are emotionally volatile and present challenges in a discussion. Among the more volatile subjects are: whether to spend or save money, how to discipline the children, who should do which work around the house, how often to have sex, why doesn't communication happen more often, how to control angry feelings and judgmental statements that lead to arguments, if or when to have children and how many. Couples face these questions often in the course of their lives together. So talking with one another becomes mandatory. But talking in a way where each spouse is comfortable, enjoys sharing, and feels relaxed, is an art that must be learned and practiced. Spontaneous self-expression of intrinsic concerns can lead to tension, because of each spouse's strong emotion and desire to be correct. On the other hand, couples can learn that by the proper phrasing of their initial statement, and by controlling the expression of the felt emotion, their discussion can proceed smoothly and promote increased intimacy. Communication without reflection and self-control too often becomes chaos. Joyful spontaneity only emerges from a relationship that is free to share amidst a mutual loving calmness.

3. Expressing Negative Feelings

Few spouses have difficulty letting the other know that he or she is upset. Anger develops and flourishes without any training, encouragement, or education. As soon as children can walk and talk, they begin to fight with one another. "Stop fighting!" echoes Mom and Dad throughout the day. Parents never have the reverse problem, where they must say to their children, "Go ahead and fight, it's too quiet in the house."

Anger is the most often expressed feeling in the home. When voices are raised in emotional excitation, usually someone is angry or frustrated. Positive feelings are taken for granted and barely acknowledged. A child comes home with straight A's and hears in a subdued tone, "That's nice, keep it up." But when his room is left unmade, a voice thunders throughout the house, "Come back and make up your room! How many times do I have to tell you that?" Anger brings people to life. Love, by comparison, is timid and uneventful.

Spouses cannot maintain their relationship for long without encountering anger. Their needs and wants are not identical in time or place; and if one spouse can obtain his or her way most of the time, life would certainly be more comfortable and easy. It is at the point where two needs are in opposition to one another that conflict and anger arise. For example, both spouses may desire entertainment this evening. One wants to see a movie, while the other would like dinner and dancing. If these needs are strong and the parties are equally determined, feelings of anger will quickly seep into the discussion about what activity to engage in tonight. Through the expression of anger, the importance and urgency of one's needs can be demonstrated, and punishment can be rendered from one for noncompliance on the part of the other.

Expressing anger in a constructive way is very challenging. When emotional energy is aroused, behavior often follows feeling. Emotion does the speaking. How often does one spouse not really mean what he or she just said? "I spoke in anger!" may be an excusing attitude. Although he or she spoke with anger, in reality his or her anger spoke instead. Anger must be controlled in the outside world. Anger at your boss might lead to dismissal, anger at your neighbor may provoke an unwanted feud, anger at your mechanic can result in an unrepaired car. But anger at your spouse, for some reason, is safe. Your spouse cannot fire you, probably won't sabotage your material possessions, or reject his or her relationship with you. So if anger must be expressed, it is done at home where it is safely permitted.

The destructive expression of anger is used to retaliate or to control. It generally takes one of two forms: an active, direct, verbal attack, criticism or put-down; or secondly, a passive, indirect, silent, nonresponse in the form of a cold silence and stony pouting. When both spouses are active expressors of anger, arguments tend to be frequent and intense, usually of short duration. It is like two bulls battling head to head. But most often one spouse does the verbal attacking while the other retreats into an icy tenseness and quietness. In this way arguing stops, but the stress of a fractured relationship continues on. Problems are aired but not resolved. These same problems keep recirculating for further resolution. But since anger does not permit a creative search for solutions, the frequency of conflict increases, eventually to the point of serious strain.

There are some marriages, by far the fewest, in which both spouses express anger indirectly and passively, with subdued emotion and a shortage of words. Needs are hinted at, not stated clearly. Fear of upset takes precedence over restoring inner satisfaction. "Peace at all cost" becomes their motto for living. Yet dissatisfactions are felt, needs go unmet, and boredom threatens at the heart of this type of relationship.

No one openly welcomes anger from another. It is threatening and uncomfortable. Self-esteem is on the line. Each person imagines that his or her life is lived so perfectly that he or she does not warrant or deserve criticism, and that the wrong committed is so well concealed that it can hardly be discovered. Anger from one spouse may take the other by surprise. "Who me? But I can explain!" Nonetheless, no relationship completely escapes from one another's wrath.

Expressing anger such that the bond of love is not severed and in a way that issues become aired, understood, and resolved is a formidable task facing all married couples. Anger is a necessary feeling, a part of the very fabric of human life. Without the capacity for experiencing and expressing anger, love would lose its vitality, its initiative, and its confidence. It takes strength and power to allow love to surface and to express it openly. The ability to speak anger effectively confers an inner, gentle power and confidence that is needed for the growth of marital love. Unbridled expression of anger, on the other hand, excites fear, not love, and promotes control over another, not control of self.

4. Sharing Positive Feelings

Perhaps the least-utilized form of marital communication is the sharing of positive feelings. Couples must, of necessity, ask one another for help or guidance, and they must discuss important issues that affect each other and require a decision. But expressing affection toward, gratitude for, and need of, each other is easily taken for granted. "My spouse knows what I feel. I shouldn't have to say it all the time." But in reality, it is the opposite that is true. Love grows by being expressed, just as muscles stay healthy by being exercised. Unmoved muscles actually shrink. Feelings of love likewise wither when they are not demonstrated in words and action.

The internalized must be externalized. The invisible must be made visible. When this happens, the love felt in one spouse is re-created in the other. Love that is expressed stimulates love in the other, and the other's love restimulates a new love, in turn, in the first spouse. A circulating flow of love occurs when spouses externalize their affection for each other. By expressing love, original feelings become intensified and deepen. By receiving and returning love, the couple bonds in momentary ecstasy. Human love approaches the summit of its capacities in marriage when love is expressed, received, returned, and mutually enjoyed.

On the other hand, unexpressed love spontaneously arises and quickly falls. Like a passing object, one saw it was there, but then attention shifts to something new. The danger of not expressing felt love is that the very arousal of that love diminishes in both frequency and intensity over time. Without showing love, boredom can set in. A preoccupation with material needs, sports interests, household responsibilities, personal pleasures, or distractions may begin to overtake the relationship. Love grown cold is the greatest danger to marriage. Yet marriage offers the opportunity for an unlimited development of the capacity to love. But too few couples actually scale the summit of love's mountain.

The reasons many spouses shy away from expressing positive thoughts and feelings are twofold—uneasiness and work. Usually, one of the spouses is less feeling-oriented or relationship-directed. He or she feels more comfortable when the mind is engaged as opposed to the heart; when ideas, plans, or tasks are discussed as opposed to vague, ethereal feelings; when concrete, hands-on subjects are approached instead of the invisible world of emotions and attitudes. The more introverted spouse can be unnerved by intrinsic communication while the more extroverted spouse requires it on a regular basis. For the extroverted spouse, communication about feelings reinforces self-worth, neededness, and self-esteem. Intimate communication makes the head-centered spouse feel uneasy and threatened. Even talking about personal experiences, let alone feelings of affection, is awkward. Intimacy is avoided or side-stepped. One spouse is then relieved while the other feels frustrated.

A second reason for shunning positive communication is that it takes time and energy. It takes time to communicate. It takes energy to reflect inwardly and intensify feelings. The avoidant spouse rationalizes that the time is not right. After a long day's work, rest and relaxation takes precedence over the perceived more work it takes to focus on and crystallize feelings. And talking is viewed as work. Since talking takes time and energy, the need to talk is often seen as a thoughtless intrusion by the other. Talking should be reserved for those times when the avoidant spouse is well-rested and not preoccupied with more important duties. This may seem plausible, but in practice, such times never seem to come. Unless time is made and spouses are willing to focus on themselves, extend the energy, and sacrifice for higher levels of communication, those beautiful moments of intimacy remain far and few between.

Yet even when two spouses sit down and attempt to share their feelings and to affirm the good in one another, a cloud of discomfort can descend upon them. Although intrinsic communication is initiated, it is often experienced as only partially-developed and vaguely satisfying. Often, one spouse talks too much while the other spouse says too little. The latter seems not to know what to say, so he or she says nothing or guides the conversation to another subject. Eye contact may be spotty. Jumping from one subject to another keeps feelings neutralized. Only human beings are capable of the most sublime moments of intimacy, yet are so skilled at sabotaging it at the same time.

In summary, intrinsic communication can break down at four points of interaction: when couples ask each other to do something, when they try to discuss an emotional subject, when they express their anger to one another, or when they try to share affection and give affirmation. In the following chapters, how communication becomes non-love-producing will be discussed in greater detail. And then ways to turn potentially conflictual communication into love talk will be explained. Couples will learn how to convert Communication Stoppers into Communication Starters.

CHAPTER IV

Stages of Marriage

A marriage relationship generally progresses through four stages of growth and development. Marriages begin in the Romance Stage, move into the Generativity Stage, fall into the Supremacy Stage, and grow toward the Actualization Stage. Just as couples have common experiences by which they are able to understand and relate to one another, so also they have unique differences in the way they experience and pass from one stage to another. As you read this chapter, try to recall and reflect on those experiences that have contributed to the development of your relationship as it is today, and begin to envision the possibilities for it in the future.

Stage I: Romance

Without that magnetic pull toward the opposite sex, that force of mutual attraction that is physically exciting, emotionally compelling, and aesthetically pleasing, marriages would seldom occur. Opposites attract. Life becomes more fulfilling and complete with these new-found attractions and excitements. The loneliness and insecurity of leaving home or living on one's own is tempered greatly by the presence of one's future mate. Life can be shared with this special someone. It is a time of optimism, unfettered goals and dreams, songs of forever love and unending joy. At this time, couples believe that these feelings will never diminish. "Our relationship will be like no other.

19

Ours will not fail like so many others" is a prevailing theme and seemingly, one cannot imagine any other possibility. Confidence reins supreme. There is no fear of a future hardship that could cause their relationship to tremble and break.

This is the time for romance, for building a union that can withstand the subsequent perils and realities that face every married couple. Many marriages fail because romance was never fully present. There was, perhaps, physical attraction with no emotional union. There was surface excitement, but heartfelt depth and openness may never have been experienced. There was the practical expediency to decide for marriage without an inner, growing, compelling sense of oneness that made togetherness in marriage seem the basic necessity of life. Romance is the soil into which a marriage is planted. If the soil is not deep or is poor in nutrients, the plant will grow poorly and eventually wither and die.

Marriage is the most profound, growth-producing, creative, and intimate relationship that is possible between two human beings. It is only in the heterosexual aspect of marriage that each spouse is brought into contact with their own depth. Through his love for his wife, a husband can unlock the mysterious beauty of the feminine side of his soul, namely, his gentleness, understanding, and sensitivity. Through her love for her husband, a wife can discover her masculine dimension, namely, her objectivity, cognition, confidence, and leadership. Within the togetherness of their relationship, each spouse becomes completed by the love for, and the responsiveness to, the other.

Any human relationship is an I-Thou relationship, where two people are joined together in time and place for some purpose. In the Romance Stage, the emphasis of the I-Thou relationship is on the "Thou." Each spouse is centered on the "Thou" of the other. Self for the moment is forgotten. Each spouse becomes absorbed in the other. "I can't get you out of my mind; I can't stop thinking about you." Just thinking about the other produces an emotional excitation. Life becomes renewed in a beautiful way over and over again by just the loving thought of the other.

In the Romance Stage, the "Thou" predominates in awareness. In this stage, the couple must unite and achieve a high degree of togetherness if they are to withstand the challenges and difficulties that lie ahead. A deep love acts as the cohesive force that binds their relationship firmly together and makes it more difficult to pull apart in the future.

Stage II: Generativity

As the marriage progresses and the romantic energies begin to abate, the need to build, to expand, and to create emerges on the horizon. Material possessions supplant emotional states in importance. Couples must put their talents and financial resources together to plan for their future and build the security necessary for their increased needs and for their vision to achieve reality. A car and home become a driving force that motivates the couple to work together.

The couple may also dream and look forward to becoming a family one day. The thought of expanding their love and extending it to another of their very own excites and awes, and even frightens them. Their love has a profound, creative dimension, a capacity to participate in the formation of new life. Their once bi-circular love needs to widen in order to encompass another in a deeply caring and profound embrace. The experience of parenthood breaks the spouses free from self-centeredness. The security and freedom to spend time and money indulgently is shifted toward the preserving of resources to care for a totally-dependent other. Sacrifice broadens the couple's awareness, frees it from self-preoccupation, and stretches their mutual love beyond themselves. Their world becomes larger. A new depth is added to their capacity for love. They realize that by going outside the boundaries of their own relationship, their love is renewed and replenished, further invigorating their own bondedness.

Like blood that is oxygenated by reentering the lungs and restored with new power to nourish the body's cells, human love needs to reach beyond itself to discover the scope of its possibilities. By nature, love is interpersonal and extrapersonal. It both centers in a unifying stance toward one person while encompassing within itself the inclusion of others. The one and the many are mysteriously inseparable.

Love is an unbroken chain of caring. The chain begins with an acceptance and appreciation of oneself. It matures as the person experiences his or her love reaching out and encircling another, whose well-being becomes one with his or her own. The chain then extends out to the surrounding community, including family, friends, relatives, co-workers, and civic companions. Finally, the chain expands out to those persons who are not seen or known, who live in the broader community of one's city, state, country, and world, who in some way call out for care and concern.

If one link is broken, the chain loses its shape and function. If there is just one person who is judged harshly, wished harm, purposefully excluded, or deliberately rejected, the growth of love stagnates and deteriorates. Old animosities must be resolved. Current feuding must be healed. Love for, not hatred of, one's enemies is the rule love follows. If there is but one person who is rejected from one's heart, then disturbance will replace inner peace, tension will replace gentleness, and irritability will replace genuine poise and calmness. Marital love is strained when one of the spouses refuses to resolve his or her hatred and bitterness.

The purpose of the Generativity Stage is to become a team, working in harmony toward a common goal. Finishing an education, initiating a career, or saving for a home add new incentive and vigor to the relationship. To achieve these goals, cooperation is required. In the I-Thou relationship, the focus shifts from the "Thou" to the "We." This enables the couple to reach higher levels of achievement that are unavailable to just one person alone. The union of romance leads to the "to-get-ness" of generativity, the acquisition of material needs and career goals. To-getness, circumscribed by the spirit of togetherness, makes this stage of marriage exciting, deeply maturing, and very gratifying.

There are marriages where it is difficult for couples to generate mutual goals and work toward a meaningful end. One wants a child, the other does not. One wants a home, the other freedom from responsibility. One wants a career, the other an intimate relationship. Each stage presents struggles and difficulties. When failures and conflicts are faced and resolved, the couple is prepared and fortified to take on the challenges of the next stage. But when failures mount and conflicts go unsettled, the foundation weakens and the following stage only adds new weight to an already-shaken substructure.

Stage III: Supremacy

Once the home has been purchased and the children dot the landscape, a new force enters upon the scene, a movement inward to rediscover and define the self. By now the individuals are probably established and settled into their careers. Maintaining the home, raising the children, paying the bills become central in the couple's lives. A routine is established, and extra energy is freed up. This energy begins to work inwardly, arousing a heightened and deeper awareness of the self's needs, feelings, and dreams. This new force is an emerging self-awareness that needs to define, assert, and obtain its way.

Previously, each spouse was more extra-centered, outside themselves, focused on one another and on their material, career, and family needs. Now that these goals have been initiated and taken root, the couple's attention can be made available for the exploration of their inner selves. Their individual needs and feelings take center stage, and seem to demand assertion, affirmation, and gratification. "I am not getting out of this relationship what I want. You are not meeting my needs. I am dissatisfied with your treatment of me." These unspoken and unfulfilled needs create tension between the spouses. Once they make their frustrations known to the other and propose that the other is the primary cause of those problems, the Supremacy Stage has begun.

In this stage, the emphasis of the I-Thou relationship is on the individual, the "I". During adolescence, the individual focuses on his or her external and surface needs (appearance, grades, athletic ability, or popularity). During middle adulthood, the individual is centered on internal and personal needs (understanding, intimacy, companionship, and compatibility). The need to individualize, to emotionally separate and distance oneself from the other in order to identify and appreciate each one's uniqueness and differences, is critical to the maturation of marriage. Yet these very differences may be felt as a threat to the cohesiveness of the relationship. To be different from one's spouse weakens the imagined harmony and cooperation each spouse had with the other. To have awareness absorbed in the external qualities of the other produces an exciting closeness. But a true and deeper intimacy occurs when two spouses willingly share their inmost selves, and freely surrender themselves to one another. Other-awareness without self-awareness leads to short-term infatuation. Self-awareness without other-awareness produces a selfish preoccupation. Self-awareness coupled with other-awareness leads to an ever-abiding and deepening sense of inter-connectedness.

Individualization, in which self's awareness takes precedence over the other's awareness, is not enough. It can lead to a battle of wills, in which both spouses attempt to change or control the other. Blame, guilt, criticism, accusation, and punishment are the weapons used to carry out this war. Who will rule over the marriage? Who will get their way? Each spouse knows that domination means more things, pleasure, relaxation, and less work. The quest for supremacy is present in most marriages.

The couple is faced with a directional decision—to return to the familiar, rebellious, self-centered individualization of their adolescence, or move into that expanded self/other-awareness, the stabilizing, self-sacrificing and self-controlling individuation of adulthood. Most couples usually explore their familiar adolescent strategy of manipulation first. Only when these behavior patterns fail do couples search for new ways to restore their faltering relationship.

The principal activity in the Supremacy Stage is to control the other. Power, not love, becomes the drive. Power is used to weaken the resistance of the other by instilling guilt, self-doubt, and fear. Power is used to compel compliance through the raised voice, the rigid attitude, the stubborn mood, and the threat of retaliation. "Not your will but mine be done" is the prevailing battle cry felt throughout the house. The emphasis is on the "I" of the relationship: what I want, I need, I feel, I like. "What about me? When do I count? Did I get married to serve you or for you to take care of me?"

Prolonging the Supremacy Stage eventually leads to a crisis. The tension becomes physically unbearable and mentally exhausting. At some point, couples will face the pivotal move, whether to end the relationship or restore it to health. If the foundation was weak and the romance shallow, ending is chosen more often. If the initial bond was strong, the need to repair and revive their love propels the couple toward the deeper stage of marriage.

Stage IV: Actualization

The need to individualize takes each spouse in one of two directions, toward encapsulation or individuation. To be self-encapsulated is to over-emphasize the importance and value of one's own needs at the expense of the other, as well as to control the other and resist his or her expectations and demands. To allow too much independence and self-assertion threatens one's supremacy. Their incipient independence must be turned into a manageable, mutual inter-dependency. "The marriage revolves around me, and if my needs are satisfied, you will also be happy. Me first." Though consciousness moves inwardly, toward the discovery of one's deeper personal needs, it remains circumscribed around the self's interests, to the exclusion and devaluation of the other. When consciousness expands from a unilateral encapsulation to a bilateral awareness, the marriage enters the Stage of Actualization.

For the self and the marriage to actualize and reach a fulfilling level of satisfaction and completion, individualization must evolve toward individuation. Individuation occurs when a person becomes aware of his or her needs and feelings, as well as those of another, and values them equally. Each spouse's individual differences must be rooted in an expanded awareness of self-plus-another. Self is no longer an isolated entity, but a permeable being that is continually penetrated by the presence of the other. "My needs are important to me, but so are yours. I consider your needs and feelings with the same attention and respect as I value my own" becomes the focus. The self and the other become inter-twined and interconnected into a harmonious blend of other-consideration and self-expression. The two become one in mind and heart. Self-actualization is awareness gone beyond one's self to encompass the desires and feelings of another and to make them as important as one's own.

Marital actualization occurs when dual individuation occurs at the same time. Each spouse is aware of two sets of feelings, needs, and ideas, one's own and those of his or her spouse. At any given moment of communication, there is present an expanded consciousness of two persons separate and distinct, but also joined in a common bond of love and concern. In the presence of one's spouse, there exists a dual consciousness, a two-person awareness.

To care about the other's feelings and needs is to care about one's self. To reject what is meaningful to the other is to cause pain and discomfort to one's self. It is as if the couple becomes two in one flesh. The metaphor has deep significance, because to hurt the other is to hurt the self. On the other hand, to elevate and uplift the other's self-esteem by praise, affirmation, gratitude, or a loving act produces a sense of well-being in one's self. What goes around comes around, be it expanding or deflating, enhancing or detracting.

Each person is made for intimacy with another. The human spirit, in its deepest center, reaches out to encompass another and be encompassed by the other. Past experiences may have overlayed this dynamic center with pain, hurt, rejection, isolation, or distrust, which makes openness to another frightening and difficult. Yet the quest for inner peace goes on until the person finds a loving face opposite his or hers, that keeps on loving and will never go away. Isolation and unwantedness are the greatest tortures to the human spirit.

The human being is made for a relationship, is sustained by a relationship, and grows through a relationship. Psychological illness occurs when loving relationships are replaced by over controlling, distant, or abusive substitutions. The human spirit then closes up to protect itself from further hurt. It experiences the world as dangerous and unpredictable.

To love takes courage. To love is to risk. To love is a decision each person must make or refuse. Not to love appears at times safer and easier. It makes sense to avoid further hurt when too much has already been received. But avoiding the risk of loving has its own form of pain, namely, chronic emptiness, mild depression, pervasive tension, and an inward unhappiness. Still, the injured person rationalizes, "Maybe I am unhappy in my aloneness and distance from others, but at least I am the one hurting myself. No one else is going to hurt me, like what happened in the past." The trade-off is one type of hurt for another. Other-inflicted is exchanged for self-inflicted. It is by being genuinely caring and loving toward another that the hurt-filled person might get the courage and trust to risk entering into a loving relationship again.

To actualize the self to the fullest extent means that the deepest part of the self must be alive and operational. The core act of the human person is to be lovingly aware of another loving presence. This loving awareness leads to sharing, listening, reaching, holding, gentle and caring touches that massage and heal broken and fragile hearts. Individualization entraps the person into a selfish concentration on his or her own needs and desires. Individuation expands this awareness to include the loving awareness of another. Self is not confined but is rather enhanced by the addition of another. When the spouse discovers that the needs and thoughts of his or her spouse are as important and meaningful as his or her own, the door to his inner core opens to a profound sense of peace and fullness. Listening is as exciting as talking.

Supremacy is not the answer. Control *over another* causes only tension, while control *of self* leads to individuation. Individuation, in turn, leads to actualization, which culminates in incorporation. The human person is not designed to stand alone in isolation and detachment from others. Rather the human spirit is porous and permeable. It remains alive and healthy as long as its central nucleus is fed and nourished by the loving presence of another. Human consciousness is localized in the head when it is centered on its own needs and feelings. As soon as consciousness extends to embrace the needs and feelings of another, its center shifts to the heart. Human consciousness finds its true center in a loving heart.

CHAPTER V

Masculine-Feminine Dynamics
of Personality

The human spirit is composed of two opposing but complementary and dynamic polarities—Masculinity and Femininity. Each is present in all persons. A polarity can best be understood as an energy field that instinctively acts in one of two ways—to invite in or to reach out to, to incorporate within or to accomplish without, to receive or to give. The masculine dimension is characterized by action, while the feminine is denoted by receptivity. Usually, men develop more in the masculine direction while women develop toward the feminine. However, there are some men who possess a dominance of femininity, while some women have a masculine dominance. This indicates the wonderful variety that exists in the personalities of men and women, and implies no hint of abnormality.

Both men and women have this in common, a polar imbalance. Each one's scale is tipped to the masculine or feminine side, out of balance and harmony with a complementary polarity. The masculine side needs the feminine to soften the harshness and render it more gentle and loving. The feminine side needs the masculine to render it more confident, assertive, and lessen the tendency for frustration and emotionalism. Self-actualization occurs when these two polarities are brought into balance. Each spouse's flexibility to move freely into their receptive or expressive mode of relating makes intimate communication possible and enjoyable.

Masculine Polarity

The masculine side of personality can be viewed as actualized and integrated with the feminine, or as unactualized and cut off from its feminine dimension. When a person is dominated by unactualized masculinity, he (or she) tends to be head-centered, controlling, selfish, and non-relationship-oriented. Masculine dominance becomes too self-focused and "other-controlling" to sustain an intimate relationship with the opposite-sex partner. The masculine-dominant spouse asserts his or her needs and desires, and if they are not acceded to, some form of punishment follows. The marriage exists, first and foremost, to satisfy his or her needs.

The other spouse, who at first resists, must be "broken" into submission. To be in control is to be served, and it means an easier life of all take and no give, except where convenient. The Supremacy Stage of marriage consists of at least one masculine-dominant spouse exercising his or her superiority over the other, superior in strength, intelligence, financial ability, attractiveness, etc. To dominate, one must denigrate. To raise oneself up, the other must be put down.

Masculine dominance can only secure its control by inducing fear, self-doubt, and self-depreciation. "If she stays weak, I remain strong. I'll let her know who's boss." The controlled spouse has little or no felt importance in the relationship. Dependency and compliance keep the dominant spouse from blowing up or expressing displeasure. Communication diminishes because the controlled spouse knows that his or her feelings and thoughts are not valued or understood. Her projects go uncompleted while his work or recreational needs are attended to. What seems unfair is explained as a priority or necessity. Resistance is countered by shouts or displeasure, coldness, withdrawal, or a begrudging surrender. The use of anger, whether of an active or passive variety, is meant to disturb and irritate the resistant spouse. Compliance will bring some degree of harmony and tranquility, whereas rebellion will merit discomfort and punishment.

Some husbands who are masculine-dominant become lazy. Housework will always be done later. "Putting off" becomes refined to an art. The television, sports, or hobbies become the substitutes for conversation and togetherness. "Work to relax and relax to work" constitutes their slogan for living. The home is their castle where they should only do what they feel like doing. Hard work outside the home entitles them to retirement inside the home.

Wives who are masculine-dominant can be judgmental, critical, cold, and emotionally-distancing. Viewing things as done either right or wrong, perfect or imperfect, they usually find their spouses fall short of the "well-done" mark. Compliments are few. Control is kept by withholding praise and giving corrections generously. Thus, the husband acts like a little boy who keeps seeking approval from his mother. Neither can grow up as long as their polar dimensions are imbalanced and unactualized.

In the majority of cases, husbands express their marital love through action, by doing what is difficult in order to please their wives. By putting aside their own needs and comfort, to make the needs and feelings of their spouse their own, they actualize their feminine side. "Not my will but thine be done." They learn to love with their whole self. Genuine love is whole-self love, head and heart together, mine and yours inclusively. Self-focused love is partial, unipolar, and unactualized. Genuine love is self-sacrificing and self-giving. This defines the essence of real masculinity. A husband, centered in his masculinity, is able to say "No" to self in order to say "Yes" to his wife. The unactualized husband says "No" to his wife in order to say "Yes" to himself.

In addition, actualized masculinity, united with its complimentary feminine side, is able to become aware of the inner world of feelings and needs, and share them with one's spouse. It is not easy for some spouses to talk about their feelings. Real masculinity is able to do what is difficult, especially to put into words the private world of hopes, dreams, fears, hurts, and affections.

Wives, on the other hand, who actualize their masculine dimension, gain a power over their emotional expression. Feelings that were once released impulsively and dramatically are now able to be briefly contained, reflected upon, and calmly discussed. Emotional arousal no longer threatens the wife with frustration because she has not been understood, responded to, or was criticized by a defensive husband. Actualized masculinity harnesses the wife's emotional energies and enables her to express them with confidence, control, consistency and contentment. With less emotion in her delivery, her husband is better able to listen attentively and respond with more understanding. And with increased emotion and feeling in his self-disclosure and sharing, the wife is better able to respond to her husband with greater enthusiasm and closeness.

Feminine Polarity

The feminine side of personality can also be viewed as actualized and integrated into the masculine capacities or as unactualized and removed from its masculine dimension. When a person is ruled by unactualized femininity, he or she becomes emotionally-centered, dependent, needy, insecure, and other-focused. Feminine dominance is other-centered and self-diffused. The need to be in an approving relationship must be satisfied if this spouse is to feel secure and have self-esteem. The measure of self-worth lies in the eye of the beloved. A true sense of self is clouded by the other's attitude of approval or disapproval. The focus is on "what the other thinks of me." "I am O.K. if you think that I am. I am lovable if you say that I am."

The awareness of self is diminished by the preoccupation of being liked and wanted. The joy that comes from just being and accepting oneself is waived in favor of the elation that comes after another's praise or approval. Because feelings of acceptance and affirmation are intermittently given, self-esteem is never enduring. It always rests on a cracked foundation. Esteem for self must be constantly maintained by eliciting new signs of approval.

Uncentered femininity seeks but fears to receive too deeply. Centered femininity both seeks and finds, reaches out and takes in, hears and believes. To hear the words of love and enjoy them is partial feminine love. After hearing love spoken and seeing it offered, then to trust fully and receive it so totally that one's heart is deeply touched and moved, is the essence and beauty of feminine love. Receptivity of a loving presence, removed from fear and distrust, defines genuine feminine love. Wives frequently wait for love, look for love, seek to be surprised by love, depend on love, but often feel frustrated and cheated by their husbands who have love to give but are too tired, preoccupied, or unwilling to show it.

Wives who are feminine-dominant tend to want but not ask, talk but not listen, feel but not define what they want and when they need it. One client, when asked what her husband could do to help her feel loved and special on this particular evening, responded that she was not used to thinking about herself, did not know what she wanted, and felt awkward at having to ask. Wives are often frustrated that their husbands talk so little. Yet they do most of the talking, letting them off the hook. Their emotional energy, unrestrained by their masculine side, runs rampant and produces a climate of dissatisfaction.

Husbands who are feminine-dominant tend to be "nice guys," easy-going, avoiding conflict at all costs. They try to prevent upsetting their spouses. They are agreeable and sometimes dishonest in little things to avoid rippling the waters. One husband said that he enjoyed his wife's cooking when, in fact, he found it disagreeable. Fear of disapproval becomes a pervasive sense of personal discomfort. Internalize the pain, pretend the praise, shun the clash. These husbands, by being so agreeable, frustrate their wives all the more. They offer their wives no challenge, no confidence, no strength with which they can feel secure and entrust themselves. They also show no depth of feeling, only a sugar-sweet facade aimed to instill a pretense of approval. Simulated but not genuine, an act without feeling, a happy mask without a real person behind it—this is what her husband has become. Conflict emerges when she accentuates her masculine behavior in order to overcome his unactualized femininity.

When femininity is integrated with masculinity, receptivity to love is empowered to ask confidently and to absorb deeply. Because one can ask, frustration is minimized. Because one can digest love fully, insecurity and self-doubt vanish. Knowing that one is loved deeply and is able to fully express that love in return centers the spouse into a poised and graceful sense of self. True beauty is found where love shines forth.

Actualized femininity means that one spouse can ask for love, be touched by that love, show a heart that is filled with love to the other, and move the other's heart to a similar experience of love. Love is the only power that makes one come fully alive and brings this life to another.

In conclusion, husbands and wives express their love in a different but equally beautiful and complementary manner. The husband loves when he moves toward his spouse to give of his deepest self through his words, glance, or touch, and is in turn moved by her enjoyment of him. The husband usually expresses his love by action and then reception. The wife loves when she warmly receives the words, gestures, or gifts from her spouse and is thereby moved to invite him into a deeper union with herself. The wife expresses her love by receptivity and then action. Her action is to reach out and invite him into an even deeper closeness. His reception is to allow himself to be touched by her joy and let his feeling intensify and become transparent to her. At this point, their hearts are open and vulnerable, able to swell with love and to be moved by love. This love between spouses is a circulating flow of inner experience and outer expression, of feeling and response. The experience of inner love must be externalized in order to transform the heart of the other and enable that love to be returned. Love that becomes enacted begets in the other love that becomes returned. Love felt and expressed transforms the spouse into a love-inspired act. When love is frequently felt and freely expressed by both spouses, the actualization of the marriage is occurring.

CHAPTER VI

Communication Stoppers

The marital relationship is nourished, developed, and enriched by communication. It also can be stunted, strained, and starved by that same communication. All marriages experience communication that breaks down before it has reached a satisfying resolution. In this chapter, nine ways of sabotaging marital conversation will be discussed. It is by knowing the particular "communication stoppers" each spouse employs with his or her partner that they will better be able to find the appropriate and effective response to improve their dialogue. Communication Stoppers are ways of talking without love. There are six ways of inhibiting communication when sending messages, and three ways of interfering with communication when receiving messages.

In drag car racing, the first few seconds often determine the outcome. In the 50-yard dash, a quick start off the block is critical to a successful finish. A good beginning means a good ending. To achieve a good start, these competitors practice often and concentrate intently. They have a sense of being in control of themselves and their vehicle. They know in advance what moves they will make. This sense of knowing what to do next, combined with practice of how to do it, produces confidence in sports.

The communication process parallels the sports process. The manner in which communication begins determines the success or failure of the outcome. The choice of words and the tone of voice are the tools of communication that each spouse has control over. By not using their speaking tools properly, marriages are unable to sustain a meaningful conversation for a significant period of time without conflict. Marital communication is often frustrating and thus is avoided. Most couples do not realize that how they start their talking to one another shades and colors, enhances or spoils, the artwork of their encounter.

It is the uncontrolled spontaneity and the uninterrupted impulsivity that tenses verbal interplay and stops sharing short of its goal. Some degree of watchfulness and vigilance is always kept over the choice of words and the manner of speaking when those outside the immediate family are involved. With one's spouse, a sense of familiarity, security, and freedom from serious reprisal enables a cathartic discharging, an emotionally-free-wheeling style of interaction. What has been pent up all day can finally be released at home.

Freedom of expression and uninhibited assertiveness are regarded as necessary virtues of the modern age. Individualism, self-development, and self-expression are viewed as psychological signs of health and success. However, action without control can bring chaos to any dialogue. Too much freedom leads to conflict, too little freedom leads to fear. True freedom means acting under control. Controlling thought and feelings, content and affect, volume and tone, renders one's messages easy to deliver and enjoyable to receive. It enables each spouse to speak with calmness and confidence. Talking is actually fun when each spouse feels fully free to express him/herself, not burdened with the need to sell, convert, or change the other. It also enables the spouse to more willingly listen to and value the other's message. Communication becomes actualized when gentleness controls expression and attentiveness encompasses listening.

In order to improve communication, a comprehensive understanding of the present problems is necessary. In medicine, all treatment begins with an accurate diagnosis, followed by an effective treatment plan. So also, the treatment of dysfunctional communication begins with a good diagnosis. There are nine diseased forms of conversing that guarantee ill health to any relationship. This chapter will focus on these nine problems in communicating. The following chapter will be devoted to treatment procedures, ways to dispel the uneasiness and enable couples to talk from start to finish in a relaxed and love-filled manner. Talking with love makes one love to talk.

There are five ways of sending or initiating messages that sabotage communication and weaken the marital bond of love: namely, blame talk, egocentric talk, wordy talk, bossy talk, and threatening talk. These Communication Stoppers will now be discussed.

1. Blame Talk

Blame talk is a common form of stressful communication. There are two forms of blaming: projection and defensiveness. In projection, the blamer is in no way stimulated to anger by his or her spouse. Rather, he or she experienced a negative feeling from some outside cause. For example, he may have lost a big sale through his own fault; or her company may be doing poorly through no fault of her own, and each feels threatened. Possibly, he just had an accident with his brand-new car; or the children would not stop crying or fighting the whole day, denying mother a moment of peace and quiet.

Feelings of frustration and tension spring up, demanding release. What better person to unload on than one's spouse? A good emotional release removes tension. And if by chance one spouse realizes that he or she is the cause of the problem, why not blame it on the other? The blamer believes that by deflecting guilt from him/herself, tension within will be more quickly dissipated. By fighting over a secondary issue, the primary cause of the stress can be concealed. To project blame is to substitute an extrinsic issue for an intrinsic one. Finding fault in the other seems easier than confessing one's own mistake. The spouse who is unwilling to feel and acknowledge his or her own guilt will try to make the other spouse experience it instead.

Paul came through the door fuming. The ride home took an extra 30 minutes. He missed a deadline at work and anticipated a reprimand the following day. Frustration and concern built up as he opened the door. "How come the house is so messy and the kids haven't picked up their toys?" he exploded at his wife. "How many times do I have to tell you to make these kids pick up their things?"

By diverting the focus to the condition of the house, and by making his wife feel uncomfortable, Paul was able to keep the spotlight off his own deficiencies and transfer his frustration to her. Instead of guilt, Paul elects to express anger. Anger is easier to feel than failure. An angry Paul is less vulnerable to exposure, hurt, or disapproval.

The second form of blaming is defensiveness, which is simply counter-blaming. "You blame me and I'll blame you right back." The defensive spouse has feathers for skin. All forms of negative feedback, even constructive, are repelled like water off a duck's back. It is as if the defensive spouse is over-sensitive to criticism, and instinctively contracts in self-protection. In order to ward off the other's negativism and reduce inner tension, the defensive spouse attacks. The best defense is a good offense. By returning criticism the blamed spouse converts hurt into anger. Defensiveness is a self-protective mechanism. Although too much blame leaves marriages strained and uneasy, at least deep pain and hurt can be concealed. And there is always the hope that if one does a good job at blaming, the other will terminate his or her undesirable behavior.

Marge had a bad day. Joan just canceled a luncheon date with her that she had been looking forward to. The children would not listen, no matter how much she yelled. Marge knew if her husband came through the door cranky, she was ready to burst. When Paul came home and immediately wanted to know why dinner wasn't ready, Marge was prepared. "If you made more money, I could have some help around here, and maybe the house would be clean and the food would be on time!" The overuse of blame talk keeps the marriage stuck on the Supremacy level, and freezes each spouse in an uncentered, masculine-dominant manner of relating.

2. Egocentric Talk

A second way of sending messages that sabotage communication is by centering attention exclusively on oneself. It is not that focusing on oneself is wrong. Sharing about oneself is a necessary part of communication. But when self-talk becomes the whole of communication, then a breakdown occurs. It becomes lopsided, unilateral, and dissatisfying. The "me"-centered spouse is only interested in what he or she has to say. He or she seems not to care what his or her spouse thinks or feels. Usually, communication remains extrinsic, dealing with numerous details about external things and events. When intrinsic matters are discussed, the purpose is to ventilate emotions and quell the inner disturbance, not to work toward a sharing of ideas and a mutually-sought-after solution.

Where me-centered conversation predominates, one spouse tends to be extroverted, outgoing, socially oriented, while the other is quieter and not self-disclosing. As long as the introverted spouse does not have to talk, he or she remains less threatened and less uncomfortable. But it becomes tiring and boring to simply listen for too long a time. So the listening spouse learns how to look interested outwardly but inwardly turns toward his own interests. He or she learns to tune the other out, pretending to be present in the here and now, but is actually thinking about another subject.

The egocentric spouse talks, not to share ideas and feelings, but to obtain agreement and approval. They do not have confidence in their own position. If their views are affirmed, they feel good. Without the other's approval, they feel insecure and doubt their own convictions. An egocentric spouse is really a disguised "other"-directed person. The reason this spouse prolongs communication and reluctantly allows the other to talk, is to minimize the chance of disagreement or rebuttal and to reduce the threat to one's inner security. As long as that spouse talks, no one can disagree, and implicit approval from the other can be imagined if it is not actually given.

Matt is an excellent salesman, and when he has a good day, he talks Patti's ear off. He had such a day and could hardly wait to get home. Patti was tired from tending to the house and caring for her ill father. Matt failed to notice her drooping eyelids and slumping shoulders. He just started in with the endless details of how he closed the important sale. Word for word, the dialogue was retold. As he progressed, Matt became more animated and excited. Patti, on the other hand, valiantly tried to prevent her head from bobbing and her eyes from closing. Finally, Matt finished and thanked her for an enjoyable conversation.

The me-centered spouse has a unipolar, self-circumscribed awareness. Matt simply did not see that Patti had feelings and needs that were as important as his own, and that by attending to her experience, he could have received as much satisfaction as if his needs were the ones being waited on. The me-centered spouse lacks emotional maturity. Just as physical maturity entails the growing up and out of the body, emotional maturity means that the capacity to be aware of needs and feelings expands and extends beyond the self to embrace those of another.

Such one-sided communication readily breaks intimacy down and fails to satisfy either one. The listener realizes that her feelings will not be heard or appreciated, so she feigns interest in order to avoid conflict. In such marriages, a volcanic undercurrent boils inside, waiting one day to erupt and spew the atmosphere with feelings of discontent and disconnectedness. The speaker, on the other hand, feels some relief, but fails to have the real closeness that comes with focusing upon another.

3. Wordy Talk

A third way of obstructing communication is by monopolizing the conversation. The wordy spouse is able to take some interest in what the other spouse says, unlike the egocentric person. The wordy spouse will even comment on the other's thoughts and feelings. But he or she requires extended time to express ideas, and lacks the patience to listen to the other for any length of time. Communication becomes a performance. Time onstage means a better chance at recognition and appreciation. Talking revitalizes and reduces tension. As in physical exercising, lengthy talking produces a social high. Just as muscles must be moved to prevent atrophy, so talking must be done to prevent uneasiness. Talking restores emotional equilibrium and a sense of well-being. To be listened to is to be accepted, and this acceptance from another determines one's self-esteem. The verbose spouse is thus other-directed and other-dependent for self-worth and self-affirmation.

Extroversion is the hallmark of the wordy spouse. The content of communication is not just centered on the self's interests, but easily focuses on the concerns of others as well. The content is more expanded than in the me-centered spouse, and includes both extrinsic and intrinsic material. Often the other spouse complements the wordy one by being more introverted and willing to listen. Since the listening spouse is able to voice opinions occasionally, he or she is able to remain in the conversation longer than the spouse of the me-centered talker. But eventually he or she becomes frustrated when they realize that their views are only half-heartedly understood and absorbed. He or she simply provides a pause for the spouse to regroup for the next wave of words. In this relationship, a level of polite compatibility is achieved at the expense of real intimacy and sharing.

Jeff had just finished cutting the grass and was looking for something to drink. Cindy, who had just put the phone down, saw him and started talking. "I just got through talking to

Phyllis. She is worried her husband may be laid off. Five managers who work in his office were already let go. They were planning to go to Hawaii in October and now she thinks they might not be able to take the trip. I wish I could do something for her. I felt so bad when she started crying. Oh, by the way, how are you doing at your job? I hope you don't get laid off!"

Jeff replied, "No, things are going pretty well at work. New people are being hired. I even think . . ." "Oh, I am glad to hear that," interrupted Cindy, "because I am looking forward to our vacation." Jeff is able to get away with saying very little. Cindy is always ready and willing to talk. Jeff finds it easier to defer to Cindy than to converse himself. She can do the work, he would do the listening. Husbands frequently experience self-reflection and verbal sharing as work. It takes energy. They would rather rest or work with their hands than use their minds and hearts when at home. Intimate sharing is uncomfortable for husbands who are often unfamiliar with the world of their inner feelings and childlike needs. Acting strong replaces being gentle, open and loving. The masculine dimension dominates over the feminine.

Cindy, on the other hand, talks to get attention. Intimacy is scary. Perhaps she learned to substitute attention for love when she was younger. "If someone lets me talk, and gives me their time, they must care." An underlying insecurity remains. Cindy struggles with the question: "Am I loved for who I am or merely tolerated out of obligation?" She wants to be loved, and tries to be loved by reaching out with words, but deep inside she does not feel loved.

In the wordy-repressed type of communication, open wars may be avoided, but an undercurrent of discontent flows quietly along. The couple knows something is missing. Intimacy is lacking. Their spark is fading. Mutuality of sharing and receiving is renounced in favor of a one-sided style of communicating.

4. Bossy Talk

A fourth way to stop communication is by trying to control one's spouse. Power is the goal, not love; control over, not sharing with. The masculine polarity, pushed to its extreme, untempered by the gentle strength and softness of the feminine, becomes obsessed by power. While the blamer spouse uses criticism and guilt, the bossy spouse uses logic and stubbornness to get his or her way. There is only one way for something to be done. There is only one opinion worth having. There is only one plan worth following. And guess who has it? The bossy spouse, of course.

Trying to control one's spouse finds its way into most marriages. Victory means less work and more satisfaction. The little child who gets its way by nagging, crying, stomping, or fighting has not grown up and learned to compromise. Give-and-take makes a relationship possible. Force and control make closeness impossible. Triumph is seen as strength, surrender as weakness.

Uptightness and tension underlie the bossy personality, which upholds a tough exterior to mask a sensitive interior. As long as a state of muscular contraction and mental rigidity is maintained, the threat of inner hurt and self-disclosure is avoided. Tension acts as a shield, warding off the other spouse's tender, accepting side. It is scary to relax and let oneself be loved, when someone has spent his or her childhood and adolescence deprived of love and filled with rejection. Prevention of further pain becomes the mechanism for survival. Vulnerability and trust must be sacrificed for self-preservation and self-protection.

A demanding attitude, founded on being right all the time, creates a barrier to the healthy dependency that two people must have on one another. Couples are interdependent in order to fulfill their capacity to love, to extend their love beyond themselves by procreation, and to give meaning and purpose to their lives. Bossiness hardens the outside in order to insulate the inside. Needs, feelings, fears, and hurts are camouflaged beneath a leadership style that does not listen, does not learn, and does not concede.

The dominated spouse, in order to maintain his or her imbalanced relationship, begins to feel inadequate and to doubt his or her own judgment. After all, both spouses cannot be right. One must be wrong, and that spouse's self-esteem starts eroding with each rejection of his or her request. Self-doubt and depression replace the earlier joy and excitement. The oppressed spouse initially felt that marriage would bring a fuller happiness than living alone could provide. Instead, the relationship has only renewed a childhood discomfort the spouse was hoping to escape through marriage.

It is difficult to continue the status quo of this type of relationship for any long period of time. The threat of rebellion and overthrow is always present. The dominated spouse has a breaking point, and if the relationship will not change, there is the choice to abolish it by divorce, or to surrender into a depression and a passive display of anger. Each spouse has a different tolerance level for frustration, which determines when the revolt will occur. If mutual respect for one another's ideas, and mutual freedom to express them is not developed and fostered, the marriage will face a crisis point—do or die, change or end. This is the time when many couples seek psychotherapy.

Bill was adamant. "You must go back to work. It is harder now with the baby and one less income. How can we get a new car and take a vacation, if you don't return to work? Besides, the benefits are good." Sally looked dejected. She had been working for 10 years, since the age of 18, and looked forward to staying home to care for their baby. "I like being home, Bill. I want to be with our baby more than anything." "There is no way we can afford it and have this new house, and live the way we are living now. You have just got to know that," Bill retorts.

Sally did return to work, shortly thereafter. Her sister cared for the baby. But she harbored a resentment for Bill that 10 years later formed into a coldness and distance from him. They eventually sought treatment to resolve their impasse.

5. Threatening Talk

A fifth way for the initiator or sender of the message to obstruct the flow of communication is to threaten the other. Induce fear to get your way. While the bossy spouse uses the force of logic, stubbornness, and withdrawal to keep control, the threatener uses anger, punishment, and even abuse. The threatener is impulsive and lacks self-control. He or she is quick to action, slow to thinking. Action is not mediated by thought, but is determined by feeling. The impulse leads immediately to an action, bypassing reflection. The threatener reacts to another in a predictable, angry manner, without the self-control that is imposed by a moment of pause and reflection. Reacting replaces responding.

A response, as opposed to a reaction, is an action colored by feeling, but chosen with deliberation. A full human response entails a threefold activity involving an emotion, the mind, and the will. A stimulus evokes a feeling, is evaluated by the mind, and is acted upon by the will. Without feeling, the human response is boring. Without thought, it is impulsive. Without decisiveness, it is ineffectual. The threatener experiences an angry feeling that leads immediately to a reaction that is often over-emotional and aimed to incite the listener. Masculine-dominated spouses possess negative emotion and decisiveness, but lack the thoughtful reflection that makes their responses gentle and loving. Feminine-dominated spouses, on the other hand, have feeling and thought, but lack the decisiveness necessary to exercise a confident leadership and a necessary influence in the marital relationship.

The threatening spouse impulsively reacts, rather than reflectively responds. The tension level of the dominating spouse is radiated into the atmosphere of the home and into the internal feeling atmosphere of each family member. Inner tension is projected outward to another, who is then blamed as the cause of the problem. A strong and healthy family is able to deflect the tension from themselves and let it return to its source. This is often difficult to achieve without psychotherapy.

The spouse of the threatener is often of a gentler, quieter, less-aggressive nature. "Giving in to avoid conflict" is the general response. The attack-surrender communication pattern only perpetuates the problems further. The more one spouse attacks, the more the other retreats and withdraws. But this only aggravates the aggressor more. The latter wants a good fight to achieve an emotional release, while the other seeks quiet to restore calmness. One shouts, the other freezes; neither calmly talk to one another. Thus, communication is aborted, replaced by a hate-filled ritual that will eventually erode the relationship.

Mark was a manager of a medium-sized company. He was friendly and liked to be organized. He worked hard to make deadlines, and demanded of his employees thoroughness and neatness. Under pressure at work, Mark became serious, worrisome, but seldom lost control. Toward the end of every month, pressure built up to meet the deadline. Mark came home one evening and just lost it. He thundered for the whole house to hear, "How come the kids leave their bikes in the driveway? I'm not repeating this every time I come home. I'm fed up. No one listens!" Mark then slammed the garage door to further accentuate his point. Carol, who had had a long, frustrating day, was stunned and began to cry. This only incensed Mark more. Unable to feel compassion because of the fury of his anger, he yelled again, "I am sick of you and the kids not listening. No matter what I say, no one listens." Anger charged the air for several hours. The meal was eaten in stony silence. It was only after three days that Mark and Carol were able to resume talking.

A threatening, uncontrolled display of anger takes its toll on the marriage. Fear sets in, distrust takes root, and the anticipation of conflict produces a defensive state of preparedness. The aggressive spouse is regarded as an enemy: "Be alert and on guard when he comes home." Whereas love and intimacy require just the opposite posture—open, relaxed, vulnerable, and transparent to one another. One's heart should not have to be protected from one's spouse. It is rather to be extended and given with confidence. When the doors to their hearts are mutually opened, spouses feel a heart-centered expansion of energy, polarizing their masculine-feminine capacities into a simultaneous act of delighting in the other's love, while at the same time revealing one's own love in return. But anger forces shut the door to the heart in self-protection from hurt and rejection. The real beauty of marriage shines forth through those spouses who help one another keep their hearts alive, energized, open, and free to express their love to one another, as well as to all who enter their lives.

6. Avoiding Talk

The listener or receiver of the message also has ways to cut off the flow of communication, just as the sender does. It is by not controlling self that the first speaker breaks off communication. Too many words or too loud or harsh a tone stifles interaction. One way for the listener to break off communication is by avoiding controversy and emotional arousal. The avoider fears his or her own as well as the spouse's anger. At the onset of anger, anxiety intervenes. There is an underlying fear of losing control. If the powerful forces behind the anger are allowed to accumulate and escape, the possibility of going out of control frightens the avoider.

The two ways of deflecting confrontation are submission and inhibition. To submit is to deny one's own true feelings and agree with the other. There is an incongruity between the felt truth and the spoken word. To falsely submit ceases the threat of an argument, even though the avoider feels uncomfortable in depressing a part of him/herself. To inhibit, on the other hand, is to know one's own true feelings but fear to express them. Verbalizing is denied so that peace is preserved. This peace is bought at a great price, costing the spouse his or her self-esteem and self-respect. Fear replaces love, compliance replaces growth, and stagnation replaces discovery. The avoided spouse may have his or her way, but the compliance is not alive, heartfelt or self-affirming. It is rather flat and depressed, designed to instill guilt without having to risk actually confronting the other. The other may feel over-imposing and uncomfortable, even when making a legitimate request. When he or she is wrong in the expression of anger, that spouse never knows the extent of the damage done or the solution to be applied.

A nonresponse is a passive form of anger, effective in punishing the unsuspecting offender and in evading responsibility for identifying one's feelings. Thus, the avoided spouse feels guilty for disturbing his or her spouse and frustrated for being denied the opportunity to repair the damage. The cold war begins. The Berlin Wall is erected. The wind stops blowing, bringing the relationship to a halt, placing it in a doldrum.

In a more functional and healthy relationship, the interactional flow of affect and cognition continues, despite difficulties and problems. Differences of thought are discussed without rancor. Intensity of feelings are communicated with self-control and respect for the other. Remaining open to one's self and the other at the same time, despite opposing needs and desires, is the essential task of loving, effective communication.

Sam was looking forward to taking his wife bowling with their friends all week. When he came home on Friday, Sue appeared serious and down. "What's the matter, honey, how come you're not ready to go out?" "I just don't feel like going tonight," she responded. Actually, Sue was uncomfortable in social situations. Her quietness made her feel uneasy and self-conscious, and less adequate than others. "I've been looking forward to this all week. I told Ted we would be there for sure. Now you do this to me." Silence. No response. Sue became teary-eyed. Sam backed off, frustrated, unsure of what to do.

Underneath Sue's quiet demeanor lies a sensitivity to hurt and rejection, and beneath that is a lurking rage waiting to emerge. She experienced frequent fighting between her parents, which frightened her. So she withdrew until the battling ceased, and avoided her parents turning their anger upon her. But in the meantime, she was denied the nurturing closeness she needed.

"You were too busy fighting to take care of me. Stop it! I'm sick of your yelling!" These words of anger never came out, held down by fear and sensitivity. But they remained in a repressed and suspended state, waiting to appear at a later date. Anger scares and threatens the avoider, who depends on weakness and withdrawal as a means of survival. Withdrawal in childhood brought protection and escape, but when continued into adulthood, it brings a power to depress and frustrate.

7. Miserly Talk

Another way for the listener to respond so that communication will deadlock is to speak sparingly. Be a word miser. Have lazy lips. Do not encourage communication, because it takes time, uses energy, and deprives relaxation. It is as if life revolves around the poles of work and rest, accomplishment and enjoyment, doing and playing. Communication is an awkward activity that does not quite fit either dimension. It accomplishes nothing and requires work. Yet communication remains a constant thorn in the word miser's side, because his or her spouse insists on talking so often. So the battle for supremacy begins anew. Each spouse presents a different need. One needs retirement, the other interchange. The spouse who wins the battle receives the spoils of victory, uninterrupted rest or mutual sharing. The word miser uses guerilla tactics, trying to wear down his opponent by small skirmishes. His weapon is the one-word answer. To the question, "How was your day?" he answers,

"Fine." Eventually, the other spouse will tire of playing "20-Questions." Pulling a word out of the word-hoarding spouse is like extracting a deep-rooted tooth. The attempt to communicate will gradually subside, leaving a feeling of discontent and an absence of intimacy.

More often, husbands are word misers than are wives. Their masculine dominance leads them to overemphasize the importance of work, duty, and responsibility at the expense of what is relational, emotional, and personal. "I come home every night. I give you the paycheck. I don't drink or go out with other women. What more do you want?" The word miser just does not understand that it is the "more" that is everything. More time together builds friendship. More sharing together builds closeness. More loving together builds intimacy.

Husbands generally suffer more from wordlessness than their wives. One reason men cut off communication by a paucity of words is relational laziness. Not that men are lazy in all aspects of living. They conserve their energy for their employer and the necessary work projects around the house. But after a long day at the office, serious talking can seem as exciting as four flat tires. Basically, talking is just more work, time, and energy and, "Haven't I done enough work today without having to do more? Don't I deserve some rest and consideration?"

His wife, on the other hand, sees a relationship drained of life, emotionally boring, and aging fast. Her grandparents in their 60s say more to each other and have more fun than they. "Is this all there is to marriage? Do all I have to look forward to is crying kids, a tired husband, and housework for the next 10 years?" A wave of depression breaks over her. A sense of hopelessness arises. This is not the marriage she dreamt of years ago. Marriage was to be a growing, daily interchange of ideas, desires, and affections that made life full and exciting and kept their hearts pumping. They had it once. How can this dying marriage be revived? "Lip-lock" has led to love-lock.

Tim had a good job, loading and unloading airplanes outdoors. After eight hours, he was legitimately tired. He evolved a pattern of: shower, television, dinner, and early retirement. Although he would do some necessary work at home, he resented it if Joan asked too much of him. She was simply inconsiderate of his needs. Joan, on the other hand, was on a 24-hour alert, and on call seven days a week, raising and tending to their two children. In addition, as if that were not enough, meals had to be prepared, clothes washed, and the house cleaned. While an army was needed, she was the only one handling this workload. Joan had little sympathy for Tim's passiveness and inactivity, a luxury she could not afford. When he sat, she fumed. When he rested, she anguished, "What about me? When do I get to rest? When do we get to be together?"

When Tim came home one evening, Joan decided to initiate a pleasant conversation. "How was your day today?" "Fine," he replied. "Was the work easy today?" she asked. "Not bad," he answered. "Do you have any plans for the weekend? Maybe we could do something together?" she asked. "Nope, I haven't thought about it," Tim replied. Joan then went into the kitchen and began preparing supper. She felt vaguely dissatisfied. Something was missing. Talking to Tim was unrewarding. He was not interested in her life. He was not even interested in sharing his own. In this type of relationship, fights are infrequent. Life just flows by without feeling, spark, excitement, or depth.

8. Objective Talk

An eighth way for the responder to nullify good communication is to focus on obvious answers, solutions, and meaning behind the speaker's experiences. The expressed-felt experience is overlooked in favor of quick-fix answers. The spouse's feelings are voided. Sympathy, empathy, and compassion are foreign to the thinker. Talk must be head-to-head, not heart-to-heart.

Common sense guides the content of communication, not inner experience. Be objective, not subjective.

The thinker wants to avoid inner discomfort and emotional pain. Because emotion is contagious, attending to the feelings of another for too long a time may produce a sympathetic response in the listener. The thinker imagines that he or she is allergic to emotion, which could cause an unpleasant arousal that might become uncontrollable. Remaining calm, cool, and controlled is this person's motto for living. Affect adversely effects him or her. In fact, it may be frightening to have an emotion intensify, because it might penetrate the surface and expose the inner self. To cry, to shout, or to blush is to lose control, which dismays the thinker. "Breaking down" and "cracking up" are not far apart for the thinker. Besides, if feelings were exposed, the other spouse might be strongly affected, and want to reach for deeper intimacy. A heightened need for, and display of, affections is met with awkwardness, stiffening, and retreat. As long as emotions are dampened, the anxiety of self-exposure is avoided.

In short, the thinker is detached from all feeling, his or her own, as well as the spouse's. Emotional subjects are diverted in favor of figures, facts, and formulas. Cognition can be outlined, organized, and ordered, and it has a semblance of predictability and control. Emotionalism is threatening to the thinker, because of its spontaneity, unpredictability, and untimeliness. The thinker has a life specifically designed around inner undisturbedness and mental preoccupation. In these people, there is comfort in areas of organizing projects, planning the future, keeping busy, etc. The mind is their home, the center of their activity, the source of their self-esteem.

The spouse of the thinker is usually the complementary opposite: namely, social, outgoing, feeling-oriented. This spouse experiences life first by an affective reaction, followed by the need to talk in order to process it. Subjectivity prevails over objectivity. One talks to think, the other thinks to not talk. One needs understanding, time, and patience to talk through the experience and arrive at an insight. But this only exacerbates the spouse, whose tolerance for emotion is limited, and whose need for silence is pronounced. So the other spouse often feels misunderstood, unappreciated, and frustrated. One wants the other's time to talk, the other hoards time to think. The result is conflict. Mutual adjustments must be made for their marriage to achieve harmony.

John was enjoying himself Saturday afternoon, reading about animal migration in the Arctic Circle. He was a long-range planner for a communications company and enjoyed studying nature in his spare time. Grace put the phone down. She felt very sad. Her neighbor, Helen, just learned that her husband had a serious illness and would live for only a few more months. Her heart sank at that news. Grace could not help interrupting her husband. "Honey, I just learned that Al has cancer. It's serious. Helen began crying with me on the phone . . ." Tears welled up and Grace could not talk for a moment. "I wish I could do something. What a horrible thing to happen to such a young family!" "There is nothing you can do," John interjected. "The doctors will do their best." John returned to his magazine. Grace walked back to the kitchen and tried to work, but she was too shocked to concentrate on cooking.

Grace found that discussing feelings with John was usually a brief, unilateral, and unfinished experience. She would find her release and relief by talking to her sister or to a close woman friend with whom she worked. They understood and sympathized with her feelings. Grace could cry openly with them, and hugs were freely given when needed. She knew John was a good man, but the intimacy she longed for with him was missing.

John was out of balance, too much thinking, and too little action and emotion. By more physical interaction with his spouse, John would stimulate more feeling energy. By verbalizing his emotions, affect would be nurtured and he could become a more complete spouse to Grace.

9. Insensitive Talk

A final way of inhibiting the continuation of communications is by being insensitive to the speaker's needs. The initiating spouse makes a request of the other for time, help, or work. The insensitive spouse resents being inconvenienced. He or she has the agenda set for the day, and any interruption is viewed as unwarranted. Doing for one's self is primary, doing for another is considered only when convenient.

Psychodynamically, the insensitive spouse remains adolescently fixated, preoccupied with his or her own needs and satisfactions, unable to experience and respond to the feelings of the other. Immaturity conflicts with the developing needs of the marriage relationship, as it enters the cooperative Stage of Generativity. The goal is not to control the other's behavior, like the bossy spouse, but to avoid imposition. "Just leave me alone and I'll be fine. Don't ask for so much so often." The insensitive spouse dreams of sitting in undisturbed tranquillity, and of having the other be considerate only of his or her wishes. Life would flow smoothly as long as it was not disturbed by the odious sound of "Do this . . . Do that!"

Peter came home later in the evening after taking an exam for his business course. He felt down about his performance. Perhaps he was not as prepared as he should have been. He wanted to talk to Peg about it. "Honey, could we talk for a moment? That test was hard and if I don't pass with a good grade, I might have to take it over." Peg, who was avidly watching *Dallas* on television, retorted, "Can't you see I'm in the middle of my favorite show? Can't it wait until tomorrow? I want to see if Bobby gets killed."

Peg came first. She was encapsulated by her needs and desires. Awareness of the other was undeveloped and ignored.

She was unable to value and appreciate her husband's needs. By responding lovingly to his needs, she could have discovered her deepest center and her most satisfying need—to give lovingly of herself to another and to receive graciously in return. When his needs become her needs, she will know who she really is. Peg will realize and experience that she is more than herself. By making the needs of the other her own, she becomes one with the other, expanded by her love, and enriched by the other's presence dwelling in her.

The human spirit is by nature permeable to, and penetrable by personal presence. The human spirit is most alive and beautiful when its self-awareness is lovingly intertwined with the inner presence of another. The human spirit is made for love, expanded by love, and fulfilled in love. Love renders two inseparably one. The further one moves from love, the more one experiences tension, disturbance, uneasiness, and disease. On the other hand, the more one grows in love, a thoracic centeredness develops, producing a deep, inner sense of peace and joy, as well as an interior energy field that is alive and giving. Loving persons give readily and generously to another, and are replenished by their giving. It is the presence or absence of an inner personal presence that determines psychological health or disturbance.

In summary, nine different ways of disrupting the flow of communication were discussed. Four ways deal with causing a negative effect in the other. Five ways deal with avoiding some part of the other's message. The blamer induces guilt; the wordy spouse draws attention; the bossy one induces submission; and the threatener elicits fear. On the other side, the "me"-centered spouse avoids talking; the thinker recoils from feelings; and the insensitive spouse avoids another's needs.

In the next chapter, ways to change dysfunctional communications into functional, satisfying, loving exchanges between spouses will be presented and discussed.

The process of change requires identification of the problem and application of the correct solution. The best remedy for a particular communication problem is its complementary opposite. In its simplest form, "do the opposite of what is not now working" becomes the stage for effective dialogue and, in time, a more loving and intimate relationship and bond between spouses. For example, talkers should listen, blamers should praise, misers open up and talk more, etc. Communication Starters are just a complementary opposite of their Stoppers. By knowing one's most often-used Stopper, identification of the appropriate starter becomes more apparent.

CHAPTER VII

Communication Starters

Helping couples learn to love to talk to each other is the purpose of this book. But too often talking with one another is the last thing on a couple's mind. It could be that talking is not a priority for them. Work, recreation, or rest always comes first. Couples, too, may find talking stress-filled and unrewarding. Why talk when conflict will be the end result?

To be successful in communicating, couples must learn to speak a new and, at first, an uncomfortable language. This new language may seem awkward, unspontaneous, and rehearsed. But what is there to lose? The present language produces tension, distance, and hurt. The language of strain needs to give way to the language of love. Talking with love makes couples love to talk. Talking without love makes couples love to not talk and keeps them centered in their perceived comfort of not communicating.

"Love talk" has two dimensions: one expressive and the other receptive. Love talk expresses itself with confidence, in a clear and direct manner of delivery. Love talk is also tempered by a respect for, and readiness to receive the response of the other. Love talk is thus gentle in tone, unhurried in pace, and moderate in intensity. A relaxed expression that is open, yet considerate, turns ordinary conversation into love talk.

Communication Starters will be related to the four modes of communicating mentioned earlier: asking, discussing, expressing, and sharing. Marital conflicts most often occur during one of these four types of exchanges. By controlling the tone and the content of the first few sentences, communication can get off to a good start and proceed to a satisfying conclusion. The first sentence will often determine the success or failure of the interaction.

Spontaneity, unchecked, unlocks old habits of impulsiveness, rebellion, withdrawal, or negativism. And yet couples feel the freedom to unleash their pent-up frustration against their spouse, when they would not ventilate with strangers or co-workers. It can appear that negative feelings which originated and developed in one's family of origin can now be safely released to their spouse without major consequence. The marital relationship reduplicates the family relationship.

As the marriage seasons with age, earlier hurts and repressed feelings must be resurfaced, identified, owned, and resolved before the couple can move to a deeper level of intimacy. The road to the positive core within passes through the forest of personal flaws, weaknesses, and limitations. Those who fail to admit their mistakes remain fixed in their own self-deception. They can only see the faults of others, not ever realizing what they are seeing is really a reflection of themselves.

Thus, healing begins with identification of the communication problem, leads to insight, builds toward individuation, and climaxes in incorporation, where two separate individuals each live in the heart of the other. Without self-knowledge, self-disclosure and self-reform, self-actualization cannot take place.

1. Asking

Just asking the other to do something is a tension-arousing, conflict-laden activity that sparks many disagreements between spouses. Both wives and husbands have difficulty in asking. Wives are accustomed to nurturing and caring for others. They are other-directed, unselfish, selfless, and often unaware of their own intrinsic needs. When one wife was asked what her husband could do for her this evening to make her feel loved and special, she remarked, "I don't know. I never thought about it." She takes care of the children's needs and the home's needs admirably well, but her own are nearly forgotten. For a wife to ask her husband to respond to her needs is to invite him to give of himself. By doing for another, he grows in love. By not asking, she fails to promote the growth of their marital love. By inviting a loving response, she grows in confidence, warmth, and openness to being loved.

"But why do I have to ask for love? Do I have to tell him everything? He's not a child, I hope. Why can't he respond without having to be told what to do all the time?" This is the lament often heard from wives. Their prince charming of the dating days has faded into a present-day couch-riveted, television-watching, rest-fixated, fast-aging hero of the past. Wives must learn to initiate, ask, and lead in developing loving communication because, in general, they are more aware of interpersonal values and their needs for intimacy are more developed. But as the relationship grows and the husbands become more responsive, wives will need to initiate less, while their husbands begin to enjoy surprising them with signs of their love. Marriage must be cultivated and sown with loving interactions if it is to take root and withstand the threatening forces that surround it daily.

Husbands also have difficulty asking. They are more prone to commanding. "Do this for me. Get me that! How about this tonight?" Where wives are often selfless, husbands are selfish. They have no trouble centering on their needs and pleasures. Including the needs of others does not come easily. It requires practice. Husbands do not want their desires subjected to possible denial. So, if not commanding, they simple inform their wives what they are doing, "telling" them, not requesting. "Honey, I am going to the ball game tonight with Bill. Thought I'd let you know." Not asking, telling. Her needs remain in the shadows, his needs always catch the bright rays of the sun.

Husbands, therefore, must learn to really ask, to be open to, and respectful of their spouse's response. Commanding and telling must give way to asking.

Asking is uncomfortable for both spouses because it resembles a child getting permission from his parents. Asking as an adult is not the same as asking as a child. Children ask for permission, out of a need to be directed. Adults ask in order to share, out of a need to express feelings and understand the other. Adults ask to interact, not just to get, as do children. Respectful interaction promotes individuation, that maturity of personal awareness that helps develop marital love.

Adult-asking has four qualities: brevity, clarity, warmth, and decidedness. Brevity instills confidence and reduces anxiety. Clarity makes the details of the request explicit and thus assures a serious consideration, as well as compliance. Warmth gives poise and gracefulness, and removes past frustration. Decidedness seeks resolution of an unsolved problem and renders communication more effective.

✳   ✳   ✳

Communication Starter: Make your request in a friendly, brief, and clear manner, in such a way as to obtain a "Yes" or "No" response.

"Honey, I would really appreciate it if you would paint the bedroom this weekend. I know you had a busy week, but it would sure make me happy. Would you do that for me?" Or, "I want to tell you I am feeling great about my work and especially about our marriage. I'd like to tell you more about it, if you have the time right now. Honey, are you able to talk with me at this time?"

Ask in the right manner and you will receive. Fail to ask, or ask in an abrupt, impersonal, or angry way and those needs will go unresponded to. Just as one's spouse is not able to tell if the other is hungry or thirsty, so also he or she is unable to see when the other needs time for talking or affection. Each spouse must take responsibility for satisfying his or her needs by sharing those needs and asking for a response.

2. Discussing

Discussing intrinsic, emotional subjects presents difficulties in communication between spouses. The arousal of a strong emotion readily bypasses the thinking process and influences the will to get its way. When two wills meet, each holding separate desires, sparks can fly, like two rams banging head-to-head in search for supremacy. Each spouse assumes that the determining factor in settling a dispute is the intensity of their emotions. The stronger the feeling, the louder the voice, the stronger the conviction. That is the person who should get his or her way. Communication often appears to be a dramatization of affect or a repression of verbal expression instead of a calm display of personal thoughts and opinions.

There are many important areas that couples must discuss and resolve. Because of their opposing views and attitudes toward a given problem, differences are sure to arise. Without discussion and resolution, the germination and growth of tension and distance will begin to occur. Some of the common areas that demand a couple's attention are: the quantity of money assigned for saving and spending, raising of children, the quality and frequency of sex, the practice of their religion, time given to recreation versus household responsibilities, and the value placed on communicating and spending time together. Unless these and other issues are talked out, problems can fester for years, denying the marriage much joy and closeness. Marriage can easily turn into a battle ground of outright attacking or into a more subtle covert operation of passive resistance and half-hearted participation. It is not unusual for couples to say, "We can't talk to each other without fighting or arguing. It is becoming uneasy living with one another."

There are six Communication Starters that enable couples to begin talking without alienating each other when emotional subjects are discussed, and which enables them to proceed to an acceptable conclusion. The way communication starts determines the success or failure, the enjoyment or discomfort, of the exchange.

＊   ＊   ＊

First Communication Starter: Be understanding of the other's thoughts and feelings. Invite, but do not force, communication to occur, and obtain a response to your request.

By expressing one's self with gentleness and consideration, the other spouse will not feel "talked to" as a child or "boxed in" by inflexible demands. If you are accepting of, and attentive to, your spouse's feelings, he or she will be apt to be the same toward you. Like behavior begets like behavior. It is no wonder that when communication begins in anger, it ends in discord also.

Steve had a difficult time sleeping. He could not help thinking about his wife's parents, who had talked very meanly to her the other day. Steve was angry. They were scheduled to go to his in-laws' for dinner this Sunday, and Steve felt torn inside. He had to talk to Cathy about it, or he might not feel like going. So he said, "Honey, I know your father hurt you, but he's your father and you still love him. But I am pretty upset about it. I need to talk to you about it. Would you be willing to listen to me right now, or maybe later, if that is better for you?"

A simple act of consideration is often enough to melt the heart of the listener and gain the desired response. A teaspoon of honey attracts more then a barrel of vinegar. Cathy and Steve were able to talk out their negative feelings toward her dad. Cathy felt supported that her feelings were not wrong, and that Steve felt similarly toward her. Steve was able to ventilate his anger and then encourage Cathy away from any undeserved guilt. They were able to visit her parents that Sunday. By communicating, they were able to feel united, become more relaxed, and act warm and sociable.

❋   ❋   ❋

Second Communication Starter: Speak about emotion without emotion. Have feelings, but speak calmly without an intensity of affect. A raised voice and loud tone turns off the listener and stops communication.

Emotional talk resembles parent talk. When the spouse sounds like the scolding parent of the past, an instantaneous defense goes up. It might be a rebellious defiance, in which anger is returned for the anger received. Blame is countered by blame. Or the defense might be a silent retreat, a withholding of love, or a ceasing of the communication. Like a turtle that pulls its head into the safety of its shell when danger nears, the defensive spouse wards off any further attack by closing up the door to continued speaking. Thus the outward display of intense, negative emotion threatens the continuation of communication.

Two objections arise. One is that without showing emotion, communication would become dull, lifeless, and boring. Those who have plenty of emotional energy and intensity can afford to temper its expression. Every word they say will be listened to and understood, if spoken calmly. The underlying feeling still colors and enlivens the subdued speaking, because the listener knows that the other truly feels what is being said. Calmness arouses receptivity. Anger arouses a closed mind and a defensive reaction.

Secondly: "That's not me. I can't act that way. I've always been emotional." Who says old habits can't be changed? If it is broken, fix it. If it does not work, why stubbornly resist change? Who wants to live in constant tension and unhappiness? It is the decision to change that brings new energy and creativity to the individual as well as the marriage. Change is a sign of life and growth. To be looking inward for new discoveries and to be finding new ways to express this ever-expanding self makes life ageless and exciting. Being the same way year after year spells boredom and spreads discontent. Not only can one change, but one must be open to change for the growth of love to occur.

Sue felt hurt and angry at John for not remembering her birthday. They were together all morning and no mention of it was made. While Sue tried to understand that maybe John was really planning something, her anger kept building. Sue felt like blasting John for his seeming ingratitude and inconsideration. Instead, Sue said as calmly as she could, "I am really hurt and disappointed that you haven't yet wished me 'Happy Birthday' today. I wish that you had shown your love to me with a simple birthday wish. I am really hurt." John felt bad and was embarrassed. He reached for Sue and hugged her. He apologized. Both Sue and John felt better. Arguing was avoided. If Sue had raised her voice and ventilated as she felt, hurt and anger would have permeated their relationship for the rest of the day.

Uncontrolled anger punishes the originator more than the recipient. The angry speaker does not like him/herself for losing control, but justifies it through the blindness and stubbornness of his or her felt rage. When emotion is present, try to speak about the emotion without emotion. As the volume goes up, the listening goes down. On the other hand, as the volume goes down, the listening goes up.

✳   ✳   ✳

Third Communication Starter: When the urge to blame or judge your spouse arises, talk only about your own deficiencies and refrain from mentioning those of your spouse.

Begin and end with yourself. Focus negative attention inward, and let the other spouse do likewise. Let each spouse identify and discuss his or her faults and failures, and not evaluate and blame the other. As soon as one spouse criticizes the other, defenses go up, and the battle begins. But when that same spouse discusses his or her contribution to the problem, tension subsides, and communication begins. Communication that is self-disclosing, sharing, open, trusting, and vulnerable is rewarding both to the speaker and to the listener. But communication that is fault-finding, accusatory, and judgmental produces a self-protecting contraction that alienates the couple and leaves problems undiscussed and unsettled.

Loving communication does not really begin until the couple moves from outer-focused projection to inner-focused disclosure. When tension surges between the arguing couple, the quickest way to restore harmony is to ask each spouse to tell how they contribute to the present problem. Often there is a stony silence. Most couples are not accustomed to sharing about themselves. Most couples become habituated to blaming, accusing, and criticizing. They have entered into the Supremacy Stage of marriage, seeking power and control as the way to restore emotional equilibrium to their relationship.

Real power is power over self, not another; it is the control of self rather than the control over another. Through counseling, the process of repair tries to help effect this transition from a surface struggle to a deeper level of sharing.

Larry grew tired of his and Laura's constant fighting and arguing. What good would another bout of mutual mud-slinging do? He knew he had a part in their turmoil. This time, Larry decided to try something different. Humbling himself, he began by admitting his contribution to the fighting. "Honey, I know that I have been at fault in our fights. Do you have time for me to talk about it?" Laura nodded and Larry continued, "I come home crabby and hungry, and the first thing I do is yell at you or the baby. I know it's not right. I don't tell you how my day went. I haven't made you a part of my life, and I am going to change that, beginning today." Laura began to get teary-eyed. She felt close to Larry for the first time in such a long time. She looked up to him for admitting his mistakes, and later they had a lengthy talk that ended in closeness and affection.

To acknowledge one's wrong-doing is hard, but to project that wrong is even harder. Confession calms, conflict constricts. Self-disclosure fosters the actualizing process of individuation, in which healthy, accepting awareness of self combines with a loving awareness and appreciation of the other.

❋   ❋   ❋

Fourth Communication Starter: Let the talkative spouse begin communicating by listening first and speaking later.

A good listener asks good questions. This means that the wordy spouse must restrain the impulse to talk, and enable his or her spouse to share first. The talkative spouse usually dissipates energy as fast as it arises. By containing this energy and allowing it to build up, the talker will develop a deeper sense of self and be able to discuss topics more relevant to the listener. Listening brings learning, and learning brings a fuller awareness of the other. This new awareness and knowledge forms the basis for the growth of marital love. You cannot love what you do not know. Listening makes knowledge possible. The talker, who is usually absorbed in his or her experiences and needs, develops a heightened awareness of the inner world of the other by making the time to listen.

Listening is done by asking specific, interesting, and self-revealing questions. The other spouse, who is not accustomed to talking very much, will welcome the opportunity when interest in what he or she has to say is conveyed. Each spouse must put on new behavior for communication to take a more satisfying turn. It is easier to try and maintain those old habits, which die hard. But prolonged conflict and the absence of intimacy forces most couples to search for the right road that will lead them both to the closeness they once had.

Sally was full of elation on Tuesday afternoon. She had returned from lunch with Claire, a friend she had not seen in two years. They shared freely, and Sally felt a special closeness with Claire. When Phil came home, Sally wanted to tell him all about it. But instead of launching into her feelings, she first said to Phil, "I had a great day, but before I tell you about it, tell me some nice thing that happened to you today. Did you have any good experience at work?" Phil was gratified that his wife was interested in his world. Although his work was routine and uneventful, the question made him look into those aspects which brought him success and satisfaction. Phil discussed the friendliness of his co-workers. They seemed to genuinely like him. He was even invited to join the bowling team. Sally, in turn, saw a new side to Phil, and felt closer to him after their sharing.

A marital monologue polarizes the energy in the speaker, and stifles the interactional flow between the spouses. In bipolar communication, a cognitive, affective, or volitional exchange by one spouse stimulates a complimentary response in the other, and the ongoing mutual exchange helps to produce a new sense of bondedness. Mutual interest in one's own message, as well as in the response of the other, creates a state of heightened aliveness. It is this balance between two polarities that actualizes each spouse into feeling a wholeness and fullness he or she could not experience alone. This balance tempers the over-used forces within each spouse—closedness vs. openness, responsiveness vs. receptivity, passion vs. gentleness, talking vs. listening, thinking vs. feeling, etc. Without this polar balance, self-preoccupation and self-interest would dominate the relationship, and an expanded marital awareness would fail to develop. It is by moderating the intensity of one's feelings, thoughts, and desires that the other's presence can be better felt, appreciated, and loved. Moderation helps restore balance, and a self with inner peace is more able to allow the stirrings of love to awaken and arise.

In the beginning, excitement soars as each person's "one" becomes "two." No longer alone, there is someone to be with and share with. One is united with another around a common bond, purpose and goal. Later, the challenge is for these two to become a new "one," such that in each spouse's experience, the loving presence of the other is inseparably contained. So from the ones becoming a two, the two grow to become a new one; that is, joined and founded in the reality of two who experience and share the one same love.

❊　　　❊　　　❊

Fifth Communication Starter: Let the silent spouse speak with a minimum of five sentences, avoiding all one-word answers.

While, for the wordy spouse, silence is golden, for the quiet spouse, talking at length is a must for communication to occur and for intimacy to develop. While the surplus talker must restrain to listen, the excessive listener must exert to talk. The willingness to do what is uncomfortable and difficult is what excites new growth and stirs deeper love. Doing only what comes naturally or feels easy produces complacency and stagnation. The quiet spouse must push to give more by speaking more words. Unspoken love is wasted love. A feeling unsaid is a gift ungiven. The non-talker has made a promise to love until death, and by speaking frugally, the promise of love sets into the darkness of unuse.

Often this objection is heard: "This is the way I was when you married me. You knew that. Don't try to change me now." Part of marriage is learning and willing to grow in love, and without constantly changing, love fails to mature. The awareness of what to change and the effort to make that change keeps each spouse alert to the love they have for one another. The question still remains, "Who should change whom?" One spouse cannot change the other; a person can only change him or herself. How often do spouses work to improve their homes, repair their automobiles, and shape up their bodies, but fail to notice their own behavior as it affects the quality of their relationship?

Esther was painfully shy in public gatherings, and with her husband she talked sparingly. But she decided that she wanted to change, for her sake as well as for her husband's. When Frank came home and asked her how she was, Esther tried to talk more. "Oh I'm pretty good. I did a lot today, the laundry, vacuuming, balancing the checkbook, and I even finished my paper for class. I sure looked forward to your coming home tonight. I would like to go to a movie, if you would like to? How are you tonight?" Frank was glad to take Esther out. The more she talked, the better Frank came to know her and to please her.

✳   ✳   ✳

Sixth Communication Starter: When speaking about feelings, connect them to their underlying needs.

When just feelings and emotions are elaborated on, the listening spouse quickly becomes restless and bored. He or she wants to know what to do in order to respond in a meaningful way. Psychodynamically, feelings contain a physiological and a psychological counterpart. Physiologically, there is an inclination to release energy toward, against, or move away from an object. Psychologically, there is a relational aspect necessitating a response from another to complete the interaction. Feelings require expression, but they find their completed satisfaction in the response from another. Feelings are part of a response cycle: stimulus, feeling arousal, expression, response, and the cessation of tension. Feelings need to be both externalized and responded to.

In marital communication, feelings are frequently conveyed in monologues, which leave the listener unsure of whether or how to respond. Feelings, disassociated from needs, often create tension instead of relief. The feeling spouse just seems to talk about his or her felt experience, unaware of what is needed from the other. He listens, unaware of what she might want or how he might respond. But when a feeling is followed by a need, the second spouse can respond effectively with confidence. "I feel sad and I need you to sit by me and let me talk for a few minutes." Emotion tied to action produces interaction.

Joan discovered her favorite aunt was dying of a painful form of bone cancer. She cried several hours that day. Her aunt was closer to Joan than her own mother. Jim came home and saw that Joan was upset. "Anything wrong?" he asked as he walked toward the closet to hang up his coat. Joan felt like crying again. "Jim, my aunt is dying. I feel really upset. Please come here and hold me for a while." Joan cried in Jim's arms. He felt close to her, and was glad he could be of some help. By sharing her pain, Joan felt some relief and was able to begin preparing dinner.

"This is what I feel in me . . . This is what I need from you . . ." Be clear in identifying what the feeling is and direct in asking for what the corresponding need requires. Thereby, the speaker will be closer to his or her self and receive a more loving response from the other. Closeness to self is the foundation for closeness to another. Love your neighbor as yourself. Love of self means awareness of feelings, expression of needs, and closeness with another.

3. Expressing Anger

Anger is a most difficult feeling to express constructively in marriage. Most couples display their anger in ways that provoke their spouse and disturb themselves, which makes the continuation of communication impossible. Anger is a powerful passion that fills the body with an energy alert and floods the mind with negative thoughts and images. The need to discharge grows strong. Some spouses tend to express this need in the form of verbal attacks and criticism. Other spouses repress the need in the form of pouting and cold silence. For some, the release is now; for others, later. For both, anger disrupts the flow of communication and breaks the bond of love. Anger, expressed incorrectly, causes couples much hurt and eventually threatens the health of the marriage. There are two ways to harness this angry force in all of us and express it in a manner beneficial to the marital relationship.

❋   ❋   ❋

First Communication Starter: Calmly state your angry feelings, the reason you feel that way, and what you need from your spouse to prevent the upset in the future.

Simply talk the feeling out in a conversational tone. The aggressive spouse will need to restrain the impulse to yell; the introverted spouse will have to reject the desire to repress. Both must talk it out, not shout it out or hold it in. The shouter must practice calmness, the pouter talking. When both express their anger in this manner, they feel a sense of accomplishment, of elation, and of victory over their lower self. Previously, they were enslaved by their negative impulses and fears. Now they are freed by their ability to simply express themselves with caring and control. Self-esteem is based on the controlled expression of negative forces, be they mental, emotional, or behavioral, so that positive forces can take root and expand to eventually govern the spouse's thoughts, feelings, and actions. Each person faces an inner battle of two selves struggling for control. The false self wants to rule by power, fear, greed, or pleasure. The true self wants to rule by understanding, sharing, and caring. In the middle years of marriage, during the Supremacy Stage, control over one's aggressive or passive tendencies becomes the central developmental task that determines whether the couple will move toward actualization or disintegration. Self-control is the foundation for the development of love, love for one's self, as well as love for another.

To express anger constructively takes time to reflect upon the underlying causes and the corresponding need, and a decision regarding the best time to express it. Once this is done, calmly say the feeling. "I feel very angry with you . . ." Next, give the reason for the feeling. "Last night, you did not serve our guests any drinks or food the whole evening. I worked while you sat." Then tell your spouse what you need in the future. "Next time we have guests, I am asking you to help serve the food and drinks. That would make it more enjoyable for me." Finally, get a response by asking a "Yes" or "No" question. "Honey, would you please do that for me?" Thus, the response cycle comes to a rest, leaving both parties satisfied and the issue resolved.

✳   ✳   ✳

Second Communication Starter: When anger is directed at you, avoid defensiveness by encouraging your spouse to talk out the feeling.

Invite anger, do not repel it. The natural tendency is to ward off another's anger, defend against all personal criticism, and display the "Who me?" reflex. Whoever heard of turning the other cheek? And yet it is the act of extending an invitation to another's anger that turns a potential bout into a meaningful encounter.

There are two kinds of expressed anger, talked-out and actedout anger. To receive acted-out, uncontrolled anger leaves one open to abuse and unwarranted hurt. This is not recommended here. But to deliberately receive calmly talked-out anger is self-fulfilling. The listener must be open to evaluate negative aspects of his or her behavior and not feel diminished by these limitations. In fact, by acknowledging one's faults and problems, a deeper sense of self-acceptance occurs, and others feel closer. Our problems make us human. Our acknowledgment of them makes us accessible. Our working on them makes us loveable, able to love self as well as others.

When anger is delivered in an emotional, unrestrained manner, help your spouse by asking him or her to restate their feeling in as calm a way as possible. "What you have to say is important to me. I really want to listen. Please tell me your feelings again, as calmly as possible." Let the spouse that is up help the one that is down. In this way, the in-control spouse shares his or her strength with the other, enabling the other to regain his or her own control. Just as disruptive behavior is contagious and spreads tension to other family members, so, too, loving behavior has a positive, enabling effect on others. By helping one another to restore their equilibrium, spouses use their individual strengths to teach one another new ways of growing and loving.

To be always in fear of another's anger is to be at a child-stage of development. Some adults are never at ease around authority figures, whether they are managers at work or a parent at home. Emotional shakiness and confusion of thought often accompanies such an adult in confrontational situations. This person must realize that because someone is angry does not mean what he or she says is correct. It is simply his or her view and opinion, and is subject to evaluation. "Say whatever you want, and I will consider it. I do not have to agree to any of it, but I will give it some thought." In reality, "I know what is really true about me, not you. But your views may help me look at aspects of myself I have been blind to." Constructive anger, given out of concern, helps us grow. Destructive anger, expressed with uncaring passion, depresses affect, brings self-doubt to the mind, and paralyzes creative responses.

Maureen was furious. The checkbook was again overdrawn, and she knew it was John's fault. He must have written checks without balancing the account, and now it was in the red. "You did it again," Maureen blasted, as John came through the door. "You overdrew the account again." John walked over to Maureen, took her by the hand, and said, "Come with me and please sit down. I see you are very upset. I want you to tell me about the situation, as calmly as possible, and let's see what happened. Please tell me about it." Maureen became calmer as she talked, and discovered that it was she who failed to make the last deposit in a timely manner.

To control or to invite anger seems almost impossible and too artificial. But what is there to lose trying something new? Defensiveness and indignation only produce tension and prevent resolution. New responses must be practiced, and in time they will become a natural part of one's personality.

4. Sharing Positive Feelings

Sharing refers to the verbalizing of positive feelings to one another. Much too often, positive feelings are taken for granted, left unspoken, and assumed they are known. Some spouses find it easier saying such feelings, but are uncomfortable when hearing them. Other spouses become embarrassed and feel awkward in elaborating on the tender side of their feelings. Developing the activities of the heart is a delicate and sensitive undertaking that requires courage, support, and mutuality. Yet the most rewarding aspect of the marital relationship is the arousal and expression of love. The opportunity to generate love in one's self and in another on a daily basis is a gift marriage offers to each spouse. What couple expresses love to one another to their full capacity or capability? Love takes time, energy, and effort, and, thus, it is easier to avoid sharing it.

❊　　　　　❊　　　　　❊

First Communication Starter: State your positive feelings clearly and then say what you need to receive from your spouse or to do for them.

One spouse may need to talk, hold, or embrace. The other might need to be held, caressed, spoken to, or taken out. The simple, clear declaration of affection cuts through the initial resistance, and produces a feeling of solidarity, confidence, and self-esteem. Practice makes perfect, and what at first feels awkward, in time becomes natural and automatic. The most satisfying words to speak are those that convey love and acceptance for another, and how infrequently they are spoken in marriages.

Dan realized how much he loved his wife, Beth, and how seldom he ever told her. So he decided to do better. "Honey, I don't tell you this very often, but I really love you a lot. I've been feeling close to you all day. Come here, I want to give you a big hug." Beth felt deeply moved, and gave Dan a smile from ear to ear.

❊　　　　　❊　　　　　❊

Second Communication Starter: Help the quieter spouse state and elaborate on their positive feelings by asking self-disclosing questions.

It is not easy for some spouses to put their feelings into words, and especially positive feelings. By embellishing the feeling with details regarding its origin, cause, and outcome, the affection grows deeper in both the speaker and recipient. Love grows with each expression. As these expressions become more frequent and detailed, love expands to new heights of vibrant aliveness. Like a muscle, love must be exercised daily through self-expression, if it is to remain healthy and growing. By helping one another, spouses also help themselves.

After Dan said his feelings, Beth decided to ask him several questions. "Honey, when did you begin feeling this way? What is it about me that you especially admire? What do I do that makes you love me so much?" As Dan shared more, his affection deepened. He was even surprised at some of the things he said.

✳   ✳   ✳

Third Communication Starter: Tell your spouse what he or she can do to make you feel loved and special. Loving actions can generate loving feelings.

The first sharing starter dealt with identifying needs behind feelings that were already present. The third focuses on developing an action that would generate a feeling of love or being loved. Spouses often do not think about what the other can do to make them feel loved. To the question, "What could your spouse do to make you feel special?" the reply most often heard is, "I don't know. I never thought about it." Wives suffer from this lack of self-awareness quite often. They are so busy taking care of others that they overlook their own need for nurturing. Husbands may know what will satisfy them, but they are often at a loss regarding their deeper needs for intimacy. When these dormant needs begin to be identified and expressed, new avenues for love's flow are opened up.

Ask and you will receive. To know one will receive love when it is asked for brings a new level of confidence to the marriage. "But why do I have to ask for love? Can't he do it without always having to be asked?" This is the ideal to be worked toward. Waiting without asking leads to emotional starvation.

Each spouse must be willing to train one another on how to express their love in a way that feels right to the other. The goal of love is to please the other, which will in turn please the self. What good is it to be pleased in the expression of one's love if the other is not also pleased in turn?

Beth felt exasperated all week and wanted to feel special for one day. So she called Dan and asked, "This has been a long week for me. I need a break. I would like to ask you to take me out to a nice, quiet dinner tonight and give me a big hug when you see me. I would surely appreciate it. Honey, will you take me out tonight?" As you might guess, they had a wonderful evening.

Candid, sensitive, clear and deliberate communication is the basis for a loving relationship. It fosters love, intimacy, and bondedness in the most ordinary of daily life interchanges, as well as in the resolution of life's most pressing and profound issues. Nurturing and satisfying communication between spouses takes work and requires a deep commitment to the deepest relationship human beings have with one another—marriage.

Conclusion

Good communication requires couples to practice virtue toward one another: namely, patience, kindness, generosity, thoughtfulness, and most importantly, love. Doing only what comes easily and naturally sooner or later breaks down communication and leads to marital distance and discontent. But doing what is difficult, awkward, and challenging makes each spouse reach deeper into themselves to discover both their negative inclinations and their positive potentialities. By admitting to weaknesses, humanness is found. By working on problems, love is renewed. By growing mutually in love, divineness is awakened. The commitment to communicate lovingly begins a process that leads to a deeper self-awareness, a fuller self-disclosure, and a satisfying self-actualization.

Communication in marriage determines the quality and quantity of a couple's love for one another. Communication can also cause pain, fear, or anger in our hearts. Communication is the invisible space between spouses that binds them into a joy-filled togetherness or separates them into a stress-filled isolation. Communication can make or break a marriage.

Loving communication requires self-control, control over one's emotions, control over one's desires, and control over one's delivery. The inner self is tempered so that the outer self might become more pleasing. Or the outer self might need to be aroused so that the inner self is enlivened. Slowing down or speeding up, each spouse must move in the direction that brings about bipolarity and centeredness. Self-control does not mean inhibition or rigidity. It means expressing self in a manner that is nonthreatening, easy to listen to, self-revealing, and open to the other's response. Each spouse, through self-knowledge and insight, must make the necessary adjustments to his or her communication that will render it agreeable to the ear, meaningful to the mind, and pleasing to the eye.

Communication must also start well to end well. The first sentence determines whether the listener will tune in or fade out. A friendly, pleasant tone and warm affect draws the listener forward. A clear, precise statement of fact, feeling, or need magnetizes attention and captivates the other's mind. A request made with consideration of the feelings and needs of the other assures most often a favorable response. It takes work for the speaker to reflect on the message to be delivered, to phrase it in an understandable and pleasing manner, and to respectfully receive the other's response. If words are carefully considered and caringly conveyed, they become the vehicles by which love is transferred to one other. Words lovingly expressed become expressions of love.

In this fast-paced world, with always something to do and somewhere to go, finding time to be together is itself challenging. Making time for communication is experienced as an ideal beyond the reach of the hectic lives of most married couples. Yet there is time to shop, time for television, time for sports and exercise. So there must be time for being together, sharing and listening to one another. Each couple must make a commitment to grow in knowledge and love of one another. Next, they must agree that if one spouse requests time for talking, the other will always accede, unless something important intervenes, and then he or she will suggest an alternate time for sharing. No request for talking will go unheeded.

For communication to continue over time and enrich the relationship, it must be enjoyable and productive. Stressful contacts will soon be phased out. And talking without any decisions, resolutions, or action becomes superficial and wearisome. For talking to enhance the relationship, it must be lovingly expressed, with precision and clarity, feeling and self-disclosure, calmness and control, depending on what each spouse needs to work on.

Instead of just sitting down and spontaneously talking, each spouse will be asked to practice a Communication Starter that corresponds and best pertains to their main Communication Stopper. By practicing a loving style of communicating, they will be more aware of what they are doing as they are doing it. This heightened self-awareness will bring about better self-control and a fuller enjoyment of the communication process. An observing, deeper awareness of self also enriches the awareness and appreciation of the other. And the use of Communication Starters augments self's awareness.

Knowing what to do and how to do it, but without actually doing it, is an unprofitable activity that yields no fruit. The seed must be planted and watered for it to bring a valuable harvest. Take what has been personally meaningful and helpful to you and practice it with your spouse. And it is my hope that your communication will make your marriage a joy for others to behold.

Talk to one another with love and you will love to talk more often. Love grows through self-expression. This expression can be nonverbal, in the form of a warm look, a gentle touch, or a caring act. And it can also be verbal, in the form of the written or spoken word. Your words are gifts of yourselves that you give to one another. They reflect what goes on in the deepest corners of your heart, the most personal and beautiful part of your self. Though you can never adequately find the exact words to capture the experience you feel, your words will echo in the heart of the other, and arouse a love experience there. By expressing love, that love goes out and transforms its recipient into love. Talking from the heart takes courage and effort, but its rewards are great. Words that arise from the heart and find spoken expression can transform spouses into lovers, companionship into intimacy, and closeness into ecstasy. By talking *with* love, you will love to talk. By talking *about* love, you will become the love you talk about. And becoming love is what we are all about.